NORELL

NORELL

MASTER OF AMERICAN FASHION

JEFFREY BANKS

DORIA DE LA CHAPELLE

CONTENTS

A RED WOOL BOUND BUTTONHOLE
ON A BLACK WOOL COAT

BY RALPH RUCCI

S trict perfection never wanders. It just relaxes for a moment to catch momentum. The integrity that evolves with it grows stronger with age.

Style and taste are part of the equation. When we find this greatness embodied in an individual, there is no explosion ... just the quiet realization that we have experienced and witnessed a visionary.

Norman Norell worked in the medium of clothes—refined ones. Clothes that look like they were cut with the sharpest razor blade and made with the precision of an architect's compass and T-square. But most of the time they were the result of an exacting construction on a hand-molded toile, in either heavy covert wool or silk chiffon. Norell, in distillation, was about silence. The silence one discovers after a great reduction of elements that went into the creation of a collection and the innovative shapes brought forth by a vocabulary of technique and design history.

You knew that you would see the most perfect and crisp, yet soft, wool jersey dresses—sometimes with a tailored wool jersey coat floating on the shoulders and mounted with a Barguzin sable collar.

What Norell did with wool jersey was original, prompted by his desire for both movement and construction, which he realized by interlining jackets and coats with heavy silk organza and silk paper taffeta.

Green cashmere suit with pale pink collar and patch pockets, worn with a pink blouse and topped with an upturned pale pink cloche, Spring 1961. Photograph by Horst P. Horst.

All hems, before being turned upward, were hand-basted with bias bands of canvas so that the roll of the fabric was determined and not weak. Pockets were all mounted by hand so that they gave a quarter-inch dimension to the body of the garment—it stood away slightly, to catch a hand moving toward the target of a pocket.

And the silence ... he would show his adeptness with *flou* through organza, chiffon, and georgette ... tucking, pleating, smocking, and ruching, often finishing a dress with a fourteen-inch hem giving it weight and balance. And the colors of his crepes, both wool and silk, were so loud that they were silent. At times he would line the jackets and coats with sequins to create a subtle explosion of light within the garment.

The mounting of a sleeve into an armhole so that it has rigor and at the same time follows the natural line of the arm is an almost religious process. Everything is in union: the relationship of shoulder, armhole, and sleeve in all of his designs is what set Norell apart as a magic engineer masquerading as a fashion designer. You saw, and felt, the garment approaching with authority and quietude—again, silence. You could not believe that it was possible to create a sleeve as perfectly mounted into an armhole on this side of the George V.

The same can be said for the hushed, just-far-enough-away-from-the-neck collars. They were molded and mounted with precision and a quiet exactitude so that a woman's chin gracefully cleared the top of the collar. Pure elegance.

Norell would show the collections twice yearly at night, thus the audience was called to dress in evening attire. A season would begin in New York, move to Rome, then Paris. Buyers, clients, and press would then return to New York to witness two showings that were known as the "American couture" collections—those of Norman Norell and James Galanos.

In addition to his remarkably wearable day clothes, there were the fantasies for evening. The deep velvets, the duchesse satin and bombazines with chunk stone embroidery, the spangled tulles, the feathered beauties, the bugle beads…and you could not focus because the sequins on jersey sirens would pour out in a range of hues: black, puce, forest green, navy, red, bronze, gold, and silver, a revolution of color and seduction only to close with silence, the quiet punctuation of gray flannel.

Norell was America's Balenciaga—he would deny the comparison. It was Norell who would flourish and tear open a Balenciaga dress or coat to study the technical marvel within, always so eager to learn. The constant learning was part of the silence of greatness.

And, this is what we have: a tradition of excellence, a legacy with no conclusion in sight, just the perfection known as Norell.

Fashion designer Norman Norell, 1968.

PREFACE

"Women can never be too simple during the day nor too elaborate at night." —Norman Norell

The year is 1964. It's a few minutes after eight o'clock in the evening at 550 Seventh Avenue, and tension is running high on the tenth floor. Instead of slipping into his dinner jacket to greet his guests, designer Norman Norell is on his hands and knees, sleeves rolled up, with a bucket of soap and water and a sponge, scrubbing the floor of the mannequins' dressing room. This way, Norell doesn't have to fret when his models change their outfits: if a dress falls on the immaculate floor, it won't get soiled. Norell is all about perfection.

The designer is also trying to assuage his nerves. In less than an hour, his elegant, pale gray salon, blooming with giant white lilies, will open its doors to a very select list of press, buyers, and friends. In a rare appearance, Diana Vreeland, *Vogue*'s editor in chief, arrives early, in lacy black stockings and T-straps. The designer's socially prominent pals enter, nod to each other, and proceed to perch gracefully on Norell's own gilt ballroom chairs. An exuberant Dinah Shore, one of the few guests not in the fashion profession, joins the front row, program in hand, pen at the ready.

As usual, the designer's pristine and engraved invitation specifies Black Tie, and his devoted audience is happy to comply. In fact, out of genuine respect for Mr. Norell, even the working photographers suit up in formal dress. And it goes without saying that everyone arrives early, because no one would *dare* to be late for what is considered to be the most important show on Seventh Avenue.

Color-blocked, bicolored silver and copper sequined gowns with A-line sleeves, 1966.

The designer is always apprehensive before his shows. He had put together this particular fall collection in about three weeks' time, and in his own mind, it was still less than perfect. Norell had never enjoyed previewing his own work, but he did love the throes of opening night—the arguments, the butterflies in the stomach, the drama, all leading up to the big event. "I think, at heart," said John Fairchild, powerhouse owner and publisher of the fashion bible *Women's Wear Daily*, "that Norman Norell was an actor."[1]

When everyone is properly seated, the music starts and the show commences with the designer's day clothes. Claudia Halley, Norell's inspiration and longtime favorite model, is the first to appear, wearing a camel's hair, three-quarter belted storm coat, a pastel jersey dress underneath, and pastel jersey stockings. Immediately, as though with a sixth sense, the audience *knows* this will be the "coat of the year." And somehow, someone will have told the tailors of America about the storm coat, and it will be copied (or "knocked off" in Seventh Avenue parlance) by the thousands, before Norell can even deliver the original.

Norell's beloved *cabine* of models—including Halley, Dorine McKay, Yvonne Presser, Claire Eggelston, and Sheelagh Gordon-Manno, who have been like daughters to Norell for years—expertly glide down the carpet, unbuttoning a coat to show

Above: Just before curtain time, the designer is busy working behind the scenes, 1963. Opposite, left: Long, lean black cashmere jacket-coat with a face-framing stand-up mink collar, buttoned over a narrow ankle-length skirt, Fall 1970. Opposite, right: Norell's green velvet evening coat, with a white mink collar, cuffs, and an extra-deep border that covers the bottom half of the coat's flared skirt. The coat appeared on the cover of the September 15, 1970, issue of *Vogue* magazine. Overleaf: The designer, putting on the finishing touches just before the show, 1963.

the lining, pivoting at the end of the runway, then removing the outer layer to show the simply elegant dress or suit underneath. Sometimes, one girl walked at a time, sometimes two, always in perfect synch. The models walk gracefully and quickly—there are only five of them, so they have but a few minutes to change into their next outfit before they file out on the carpet again. Meanwhile, the buyers and editors and ladies are scribbling away on their pads, noting their favorite numbers.

When the first half of the show is over, the lights go up for intermission. There is a buzzy, genial mood among the audience. Champagne is poured, pleasantries are exchanged, and, after a short while, the nighttime Norells will emerge with dresses full of drama, sophistication, sparkle, and shine.

At show's end, the audience surges to its feet for a standing ovation and Norell, totally exhausted, is pushed by his models out into the lights, in his shirtsleeves, "tired, haggard, and happy *only* if he has pleased."[2] He has most definitely pleased.

Notes
1. John Fairchild, *The Fashionable Savages* (New York: Doubleday, 1965), 94.
2. Ibid., 96.

INTRODUCTION

Norell admiring model Yvonne Presser, during her final show before retirement, in a dramatic silver sequin dress with white floor-length coq feather coat, 1970.

Born in the first year of the twentieth century, Norman Norell was a true pioneer in the American fashion industry. As it turned out, Norell would be many firsts for an American designer: the first to have his own name on a dress label, the first to have his name on his own fabulously successful fragrance, and the first to make clothes whose quality was truly on par with Paris couture.

Early in his career, under the tutelage of fashion entrepreneur Hattie Carnegie, Norell absorbed everything he needed to know about meticulous cut, fit, and quality fabrics. His twice-yearly trips to Paris with Carnegie allowed him to experience the standards of couture that made French clothes the epitome of high fashion. Norell developed the unique ability to translate the characteristics of couture into American ready-to-wear. Learning to inspect each garment individually and carefully, in the mode of a couturier, he grew to demand proper fabrication and finish.

When the famed French couture houses were shuttered during the Second World War, Norell customized his designs to the American taste. Anticipating the government's restrictions on fabric yardage, Norell coolly brought back the sheath dress, a classic shape from the 1920s, which remained popular for the next twenty years.

Early on, Norell began to develop certain design characteristics that remained with him throughout his nearly fifty-year career. He introduced demure wool jersey shirtwaist dresses with bowed collars—a far cry from the overly splashy, flowered day dresses of the 1940s.

When Norell turned to evening clothes, he was able to hark back to the flashy and glamorous days when he made costumes for vaudeville. Happily for the designer, the wartime fabric restrictions did not pertain to the glittering paillettes (sequins), which were not made of metal and therefore not rationed. Paillettes were sprinkled on skirts or coats for a soupçon of flash, and later, Norell would go all out, covering a whole dress with the sequins as he did in his famous mermaid evening dresses. To be noted, the sequins were sewn on, one by one, by hand.

Norell took pride in having introduced the plain (not draped) neckline, which de-cluttered a dress, allowing for a more modern line. His suits were marvels of simplicity, in neutrals and also clear Crayola colors. Patterns were used minimally, using only polka dots, checks, and stripes—one of the ways he made the wearer the focus of attention.

The haberdashery his father owned influenced Norell to the adaptability and practicality of menswear. He designed a no-nonsense but feminine uniform consisting of a sleeveless jacket or vest over a bowed blouse and a slim wool skirt, which was far more comfortable than a jacket with sleeves.

Norell's clothes were often copied, both domestically and across the sea. Paris flipped over his fourteen-gore ice-skating skirt, which was knocked off by many. When Norell designed his famous culotte suit, he offered working sketches of the pattern free to the trade to make sure that it would be copied correctly. This kind of integrity earned him a place as the foremost designer of his time and, with it, the Seventh Avenue garment industry gained new global respect.

Opposite: Traina-Norell's charmingly inventive strapless summer dresses in black or white, with curved cuffs that can be added to the arm to create an alternative silhouette, Spring 1950. Photograph by Louise Dahl-Wolfe. Overleaf: Multiple images of Dorian Leigh in black and/or white. From left, white cotton dance dress, slinky black sheath, and sleek black dress with white tuxedo bib overblouse and exaggerated cuffs, 1950. Photographs by Gjon Mili.

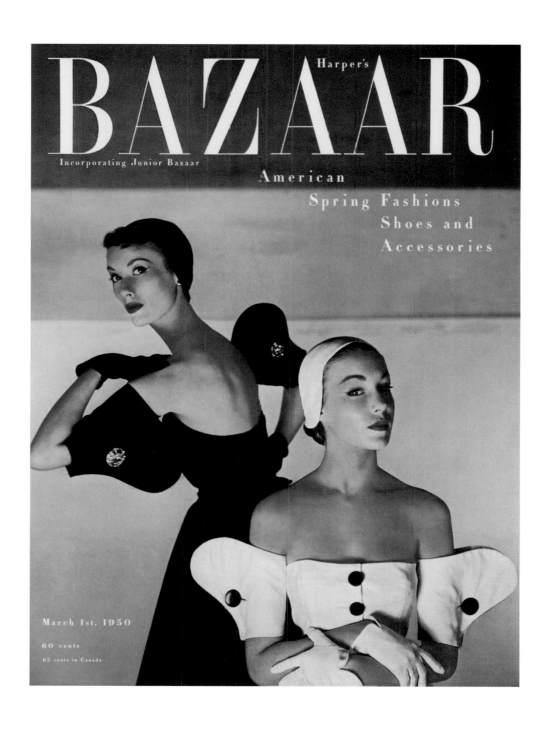

PART I: THE CLOTHES

Norell's smart theater suit: a vicuna-colored camel's hair jacket lined with matching paillettes and worn over a sleeveless pailletted mermaid top and slim floor-length skirt, mid-1960s. Norell enjoyed using the surprise element of a lining with paillettes.

Norman Norell (1900–1972) was as talented at designing day dresses as he was at creating elegant evening clothes. This versatility was unusual among designers of his time, most of whom were more skilled at one specialty or the other. Norell's superbly tailored coats, suits, dresses, knits, and woven chemises were so simple and well made that they remained fashionable for years and lasted forever, making him the first American designer to win the respect of the Paris couturiers.

Norell developed certain outstanding trademarks at the beginning of his nearly five-decades-long career, and, creature of habit that he was, those trademarks remained a constant. He made endless versions of his simple wool jersey dresses that were serious and smart: with the classic combination of clean lines and soft tailoring, the dress just lightly skimmed the body at bust, waist, and hips. Both feminine and refined, the well-mannered wool jersey dress performed well from morning to night. It became a sure winner that went on for decades, with only the most minimal changes of buttons, belts, or skirt length. Over the years, the designer sold thousands of these dresses, and his devotees always clamored for more.

Norell's knit chemises were perfection: perennial best sellers with a flattering fit for almost any body and the ability to be worn anywhere, they were the mainstays of the designer's collection. The dresses were made in several different weights of Racine jersey and often formed the core of a woman's Norell wardrobe. On a simple black chemise, the designer might choose to use a contrasting color like blue for the working buttonholes to add a little pizzazz.

Above: Fitted, gray fox–
trimmed greige bolero,
buttoned over a matching
sleeveless greige wool
dress, bordered with gray
fox at the hem, 1967.
Drawing by Michael
Vollbracht. Opposite: On
the left, a 1920s-inspired,
boxy beige jersey jacket,
lined edge-to-edge with
black-and-beige stripes
and worn over a slim black
skirt. At right, a beige wool
jersey tunic, belted with a
narrow black belt, over a
knife-pleated skirt, 1964.

Although his designs were simple and spare in line, Norell loved to decorate his clothes with shine and sparkle. The designer doted on the most luxurious trimmings: furs such as sable and mink to border a skirt, neckline, jacket, or edge of sleeves; beading, bugles, and his favorite, sequins, which were flat-stitched by hand, one at a time, to a chain—three stitches per sequin—to secure them properly. Beaded silk crepe, chiffon, organdy, wool jersey, wool, and linen were also employed. One fanciful dress was done in crepe, with sequins graduated from hem to thigh, each sequin bearing a single ostrich feather in the center. The designer used mock diamonds often on knits, and on double-knit pink chemises, he added clusters of faux rubies to help hold the shape of the dress's hem.

There were a number of classic shapes that Norell loved, reworked, and refined over the years: A-line dresses with sleeves cut high and narrow; nautical dresses with sailor collars; jumpers; empire-line dresses that one season were long in gold lamé, and the next season were black wool with puffed sleeves. He used dolman sleeves on evening gowns and, knowing that they were a hard sell, he cut them not from the waist but halfway between the waist and shoulder, so they wouldn't be quite as full. He adored the idea of evening gowns in wool—some short, some beaded, some bordered with glorious sable or fox.

Traina-Norell's forest-green
chiffon ankle-length dress
with a ripple of mink at the
neckline, which culmi-
nates in a nosegay of pale
pink roses, Fall 1952.
Photograph by Horst P.
Horst. Lauren Bacall wore
this dress in the 1953
movie *How to Marry a
Millionaire*.

Opposite: Black and gold sequins form a giraffe print on a slinky, low-backed chemise, mid-1960s.
Right: Elegant and refined, Norell's bugle-bead-and-pearl-embroidered, sleeveless, empire-waisted dress, wrapped with a wide silk satin bow, 1963.

SAILOR DRESSES

In the early twentieth century, children often wore crisp little sailor suits: boys with a middy top and shorts and girls in full-skirted dresses. Norell, who grew up in classic Peter Thomson sailor suits, was keen on nautical dresses for women, often with giant billowing skirts and full sleeves—or sometimes simply sleeveless with a beautifully cut, nearly bare back. In keeping with the nautical touch, there was always a bow of heavy silk, lined in organdy to keep it shipshape.

One of Norell's forever classics: a crisp white cotton organdy sailor dress, with billowing sleeves and a ballroom skirt, banded with navy satin at the collar, wrists, and hem, cinched with a navy belt, and tied with a beautiful red satin bow, Spring 1968.

Above: Yvonne Presser
whirls on the runway in
Norell's ultra-feminine
white, red, and blue,
seaworthy summer dress.
Opposite: Perfect from
every angle, Norell's nautical dress sports a squared-
off, navy-trimmed collar, a
navy belt, and a navy ribbon
circumnavigating the hem
of the wide ballroom skirt,
Spring 1968.

LITTLE BLACK DRESSES

Devastatingly pretty and sexy, Norell's little black dress was the kind that women loved to wear. The dress's neckline and armholes were always faced to keep the garment shapely and give it body. The wool fabric was light but spongy. The edge of the neckline and armholes were under-pressed, a procedure that prevented seams from showing on the outside, as were the hems, which were lined with bias-cut organdy, endowing the dress with a beautiful edge.

The ultimate Little Black Dress: Black jersey bodice clean-lined and beautifully cut with its round neckline, just covering the clavicle; narrow waist; and simple, bell-shaped black tweed skirt, early 1960s.

Norell's sumptuous wool three-quarter sleeve topper, in absinthe yellow, over a sleek black jersey sheath, Spring 1961. Photograph by Horst P. Horst.

EVENING ATTIRE

A Norell evening gown was often done in three distinct colors: one for the top, one for the skirt, and another for the sash. A double layer of fabric was used to give the sash more heft, and sometimes leather was used for lining. The designer used a contrasting color for a silk sash that was trimmed at the outer edges in gold thread or a softer silk-satin binding.

Norell originated the idea of using traditional sportswear elements for his evening dresses: cardigan jackets, jersey turtlenecks, trousers, and tank tops were treated to sparkling sequins, organdy, and faille. The designer loved contrast, a kind of high/low American mix that made evening clothes both glamorous and sportive at the same time.

Traina-Norell's crimson velvet top worn with a white, heavy duchesse satin ball skirt, wrapped with a giant bow, Fall 1956. Photograph by Horst P. Horst.

Page 46: Dark brown
faille evening gown w th
bustle-back skirt. The
stole is bound with a
double band of white
mink, 1965. Drawing
by Kenneth Paul Block.
Page 47: Jean Patchett in
Traina-Norell's pistachio
duchesse satin gown
and matching Barguz n
sable–trimmed wrap, Fall
1948. Photograph by John
Rawlings. Opposite: Sultry,
skinny-strapped stunner in
black, with long, silky fringe
for Traina-Norell, Fall 1952.
Photograph by Irving Penn.

FULL, FABULOUS SKIRTS

Norell was mad about full, feminine dirndls—a favorite skirt shape that he used in different widths, from gently pleated to giant balloon shapes. For evening skirts, he would exaggerate and use three layers of tulle, each one stitched with horsehair to stand out even further. The skirts were channel-stitched and graduated and, as with everything he did, they had body and volume while seeming to be weightless. Norell loved to pair voluminous evening skirts of silk satin with a pleated blouse, silk jersey turtleneck, or, by the late 1960s, a cashmere turtleneck.

The ultimate ball skirt: Black and ivory striped duchesse satin lavished with a black fox hem, belted in trapunto-stitched pink satin, and topped with black silk jersey turtleneck, Fall 1967.

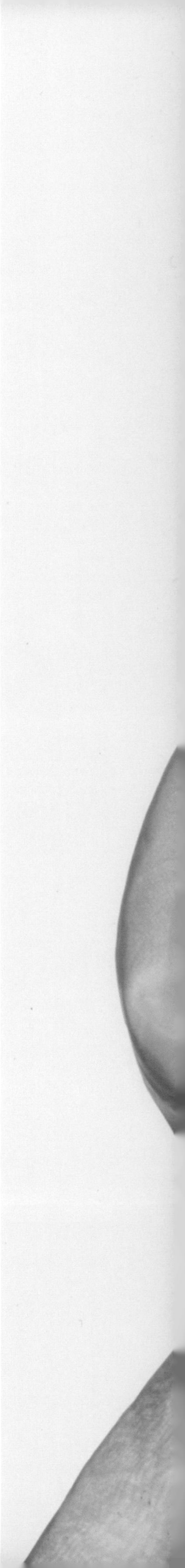

Lauren Hutton wears
a bright citron cotton
organdy dress with Norell's
favorite bouffant sleeve,
belted in white leather,
Spring 1968. Photograph
by Irving Penn.

MERMAID GOWNS

These gorgeous gowns were clearly influenced by Norell's early work designing show business clothing for both Brooks Costume Company and Paramount Pictures in Astoria, Queens, where a number of silent moviemakers and theatrical companies were located. The gowns were guaranteed showstoppers whether sequined, beaded, or wrapped in faux rubies, and they all became Norell classics. The sequined dresses embodied the balance that Norell strived for: a meld of flashiness and simplicity. The mermaid madness started in the 1930s and continued through the end of Norell's career.

Empire-waisted purple sequined dress to the floor, mid-1960s.

Norell's silver beauty, with hand-sewn alternating bands of sequins on a mermaid dress in silk jersey to the floor, Fall 1966. Photograph by Horst P. Horst.

FANTASY COATS

Norell's fabulous collection of coats were covered with giant pink and red roses, fluttering ostrich feathers, or brilliant coq feathers in a fiery orange that would match the sequined dress underneath. These were the runway stunners—the model would glide through the room and open her feathery or flowery coat to reveal a very sexy wool crepe bias halter dress with plunging neckline.

Opposite: Claudia Morgan in a harem-hemmed chiffon divided dress and over-the-top ostrich cape, with Norell seated below, 1960. Overleaf: Norell's canon of clothes is exhibited, including an audacious mix of tweed and sequins, sophisticated cuts, feathered coats, feminine fur trims, strong and vibrant colors, and most of all the sleek silhouettes of his favorite period, the 1920s. All from his spectacular Fall 1960 collection. Photograph by Milton H. Greene.

Fantasy coats: fluttery, feminine, and full of glamour. Above: Mrs. Max Fisher in a whimsical white coat abloom with pink, red, and purple anemones, Spring 1967. Drawing by Michael Vollbracht. Opposite: Norell loved to design evening coats with enormous hand-dyed silk organza flowers or fiery colorful coq feathers, an example shown here over a sequined mermaid dress, 1971.

THE INFLUENCE OF MENSWEAR

Since his family owned and operated a successful haberdashery for many years, Norell was exposed early on to the fabrics and cuts and details of traditional menswear. There is a logic and inherent practicality in men's clothing, whereas womenswear was often designed to be more decorative than functional. So Norell set out to combine the concepts, designing beautifully fitted women's clothes that embraced the notion of menswear practicality. His sleeveless jackets for women, to be worn with a feminine bowed blouse and a slim woolen skirt, provided both a comfortable fit and a crisp professional look.

In the 1950s, women were not yet wearing pants at the office, and in 1960, when the designer launched his own label, he created excitement with his culotte suit in wool flannel. Sophisticated women welcomed the ease and movement allowed by Norell's so-called divided skirt. A few years later, Norell designed a black dinner suit with a bow tie for a woman, which was a big success at the time and predated Yves Saint Laurent by a decade. He borrowed velvet-collared Chesterfield coats and tweed reefers from the men, and women were thrilled to have them. Later in the 1960s, Norell designed his first women's version of the jumpsuit, which started out as a lightweight aviator's garment; the menswear-influenced one-piece outfit was usually made of silk or other soft, luxurious fabric for evening wear.

Norell appreciated the fact that men's clothing had historically been very slow to change, but he began to see how he could use his own designs for women over and over again, while he continuously tweaked and refined them in keeping with the times.

Designer deities: Norman Norell and Yves Saint Laurent walking in New York,1965.

Above: Traina-Norell's
revival of a cropped, quilted
Victorian vestee worn over
a short-sleeved mono-
chrome wool dress, deco-
rated with antique diamond
pins and a flat-topped hat
with elegant feather, early
1940s. Opposite: Black
and white linen vests worn
over short-sleeved jersey
dresses from Traina-Norell,
Spring 1946. Photograph
by John Rawlings.

Above: Norell's sharply
defined white Honan silk
pantsuit, Spring 1972.
Photograph by Irving Penn.
Opposite: An abbreviated
red gabardine faux-fur-lined
storm coat by Traina-Norell,
Fall 1943. Photograph by
John Rawlings.

Above: Double-breasted, short-jacketed wool twill culotte suit, Fall 1960. Drawing by Kenneth Paul Block. Opposite: Norell's headline-making Donegal tweed tailleur with dirndl culottes, which sent shock-waves through the fashion world from his 1920s-inspired collection, Fall 1960. Photograph by Milton H. Greene.

Above: Black-and-white
houndstooth double-
breasted wool pantsuit
with red-and-white polka-
dot bow blouse, Spring
1969. Drawing by Michael
Vollbracht. Opposite:
Loden-green and purple
tartan-plaid wool pantsuit
with ivory jersey turtleneck,
Fall 1971. Photograph by
Gianni Penati.

Above: Double-breasted
women's balmacaan coat
of checked fabric featuring
a flat collar, raglan sleeves,
and welt pockets, 1965.
Drawing by Norman
Norell. Opposite: Prince of
Wales tweed reefer coat
with martingale back and
mother-of-pearl buttons,
late 1960s.

NORELL'S CLOTHES WERE AS GOOD ON THE INSIDE AS THEY WERE ON THE OUTSIDE

t's often been said that Norman Norell was something of a genius in the world of fashion. His brilliance and taste in every part of the process—design, fabrication, construction, tailoring, and fit—were without parallel. But perhaps his most remarkable skill was his least obvious: the inner construction of a garment, the unseen framework that forms and shapes a dress or coat or ball gown into a bona fide Norman Norell. "He has an engineer's mind," said Wilson Folmar, a fellow Seventh Avenue designer. The interior, according to Norell, is often the secret of a dress's success.

For Norell the perfectionist, cut and proportion, construction and shape were of the highest importance. That is why his sell-through at retail was consistently excellent. In his shop, one highly experienced patternmaker made every single chemise, because he fully understood the characteristics of knits and their relationship to shape. The designer demanded meticulous work: all of his seams were two inches or deeper. In today's world, there is virtually no seam allowance in even the most expensive clothes. In Norell's era, pants were fully lined so the knees and seat did not bag out and the garment was always able to keep its shape; today, pants are only lined in the front, if at all.

Norell abhorred bust darts, asserting that they were the mark of "home sewers." He did everything possible to avoid using them, instead employing princess seams, multiple gores, and empire seaming. His two-piece jacket sleeves were a marvel of engineering, with the under-sleeve panel being slightly off grain so as to allow for ease of movement without the "dreadful" darts. All of his garments' stock was under-pressed,

Watermelon-pink piqué
heavy wool jersey dress
with self-fabric belt,
Spring 1966.

a technique that was often used by other designers for samples, but rarely utilized for stock. Not so for Mr. Norell: he was willing to go to great lengths to create a couture-like quality for his clothes.

The designer definitely had his own ideas about his cuts: he fervently believed a woman's clavicle should be covered with fabric in front and slightly dipped in back, to elongate the neck. He was very fond of neat Peter Pan collars, soft pussycat bows, cheongsam banded-neck chemises, and turtlenecks on dresses and blouses.

According to Norell, in addition to concealing the clavicle at the base of a woman's neck, the fabric covering the armpit, where a woman's fleshy area might show, should be cut high. For a sleeveless dress, the fabric was always extended out to the edge of the shoulder for a more flattering line, and a spongy, light wool with facing softened the area around the arm. Dresses—especially wool jersey evening gowns with plunging necklines to the waist—were always cut close to the body so the bosom was contained at the front and side. With Norell, modesty prevailed!

Above: Detail of a sheath dress, showing vertical fold of fabric subtly turning into armhole facing and tacked by hand, eliminating the need for bust darts, which Norell abhorred. Opposite: Inside detail of side zipper on nutmeg tweed dress, mid-1960s. The zipper was only visible on the bodice to the waist; the rest of the zipper was left free to float inside the pocket, eliminating the need for a very long zipper down the side of the dress.

All of Norell's cuts were made to camouflage and enhance a woman's body. The designer always cut his dresses to cover the breast and the area between the breast and the arm, as in a halter neckline, and straps or bare-back straps were placed to support the bosom like a bra. Norell was fine with women wearing a bra with his clothes, but only if it didn't show: there were always stays for support.

While Norell was working for Hattie Carnegie early in his career, he met and befriended Miriam Abrams, a talented designer in her own right. After Norell left Carnegie and subsequently formed a partnership with Anthony Traina, Miriam became one of his best customers; years later, when Norell established his own business, she would bring her young son, Lawrence, with her to the showroom. Encouraged by Norell himself, Lawrence ultimately became a designer. The insights Lawrence gained into Norell's meticulous methods of inner construction shed light on the reasons why Norell's clothes looked as good on the inside as they did on the outside.

Above: Norell's deceptively simple pink silk crepe obi dress, Spring 1965, had a built-in bardeau with hook-and-eye front closure, allowing for the outer layers to smoothly wrap the bust. Opposite: Inside Norell's camel's hair skirt, the deep hem and facing were bound in silk and hemstitched by hand. Note the Norell label on the skirt's back vent. Overleaf: Norell's ivory wool sheath evening dress made without any darts (left); pale beige cashmere pea jacket with satin piping over the same sheath (right), both Fall 1964.

300

1148/
15

MATERIAL GUY

Norell's first step in creating was to select the fabric—a task that he wouldn't have dreamed of delegating to anyone else. He said, "I close my eyes, squash a piece of coating around in my hand, feel its heft, solidness. Good fabric has good weight. It has a reason."[1]

During the war years, fabrics from France and Italy had not been available, but once Europe was back on its feet, Norell made a point of sourcing his fabrics from the finest houses in France and England: Racine for wool jerseys and Linton Tweeds from Great Britain (both suppliers of Chanel). Postwar, Norell bought Abraham silks from Zumsteg in Switzerland; silks from Gandini and cashmere and alpaca from Agnona in Italy; and vicuña from South America—then the most expensive fabric in the world, at one hundred dollars per yard. Norell also invested in superb fabrics such as chiffon from Bianchini; silk from Staron; wools from Dormeuil; tweeds and wools from Nattier; Italian wools, silk tweeds, and worsted wool from Petillaut; and linen from Moreau.

His suits and coats have such substance and shape that they appear to have a form within them, even on a hanger. To achieve this, one would think that Norell needed an abundance of interfacing, underlining, and padding, but he used only a lightweight linen wigan (a stiff, canvas-like fabric), which added stability rather than shape. He used hair canvas only for the upper collar, where the pad stitching was surprisingly widely spaced. It was the wool fabric, spongy double cloth, melton, gabardine, and heavy cavalry twill—modeled to shape with a flat iron wrapped in damp linen towels—that gave Norell coats and suits their distinctive resilience.[2]

Coat with the designer's famous Puritan collar, Fall 1968. Sketch by Norman Norell.

Above: Sable-collared
double-breasted belted
wool coat with matching
sable muff, late 1960s.
Sketch by Norman Norell.
Opposite: Ultra-fitted
mink-collared cavalry twill
double-breasted coat with
patch pockets and horn
buttons, late 1960s.

The sophisticated clothes that Norell designed were treated with great respect: suits and jackets and sleeves were lined when necessary, and double-faced satin dresses were lined in silk organdy and then silk. There were different grades of organdy for the linings. Facings were important: a jersey blouse was faced with organdy; the yoke of the blouse had silk seams, bound in silk piping or chiffon. Tweeds were always bound. Norell wanted seams and waistbands to be thin, but never bulky. Jackets were lined in taffeta or satin; coats, always satin. Different weights were used to keep the garment's shape and lightness. Delicate chiffon was hard to stitch, so the designer used tissue paper while seaming. When he was in the process of cutting, he would hang up the chiffon so it couldn't stretch; afterward, it was hand-stitched.

Norell's belts, whether wonderfully slim or five inches wide, belted high or just grazing the hip bone, were always crafted by the fastidious Ben King. Worked in leather, suede, or self-fabric, they were often stitched with neat rows of channel stitching. Norell's belts always cinched a dress or suit with a flattering, finished look.

Norell's dresses were most often worked in wool jersey. Fluid yet with a definite character, the fabric conformed to his premise that a woman's body movement should be seen under the dress, but any hint of tightness was unacceptable. Once again, Norell achieved his shaping with the lightest interfacings—linen or silk organza—for which he sometimes paid twenty dollars per yard. To get the proper weight for an elegant drape in these jersey dresses, he didn't hesitate to use ten-inch interfaced hems. Norell liked to use contrast colors for buttonholes on his knit chemises, such as a black dress with red thread. Suit blouses and jacket linings were in silk prints. Jersey dresses had silk yoke facing, organdy yoke, and over-seams bound in silk piping. Hems of the jersey dresses were at least four to six inches deep. All buttonholes were covered in taffeta; all zippers were set by hand. When asked about his extravagance, Norell would always reply that he was unable to compromise, and that it was too late for him to change.[3]

Dirndl skirts were always lined in stiff taffeta to make them stand out; a slim skirt would have been lined in soft silk to help keep the shape; pockets had little metal discs or chains to keep them flat. All buttons on jacket sleeves were fully functional.

Norell's suits, subtle and simply flattering, called attention to the women wearing them rather than to the clothes themselves, and that's the way the designer always wanted it to be. He had a wonderful eye for color, preferring clear solid colors: black, beige, red, bright orange, and light blue, which he often adorned with large contrasting buttons. His use of pattern was limited, and apart from the occasional stripes, checks, and polka dots, he was true to his clear, sophisticated solids.

Summer was the least important season at Norell because of his high price points, so he would take his best-selling gowns from fall and "knock off" his own shapes, doing them in sorbet shades in linen, jazzing them up with beading here and there. On the other hand, Cruise/Holiday in the winter season was one of the high points and exceedingly important. The designer himself, along with his models, would fly down to renowned retailer Martha in Palm Beach to personally sell his clothes to his warm-weather customers.

For fall and spring, Norell went to Paris for fabrics, and while he was there would sometimes go to the houses of Balenciaga, Givenchy, and Chanel to take a good look at the designers' techniques and workmanship. He conceded that he was somewhat influenced by Balenciaga's technique and cuts, but Norell never copied. He was true to himself and always chose to rework his own favorite silhouettes.

Midi suit with bolero jacket and asymmetric, buttoned slide slit, Spring 1968. Sketch by Norman Norell.

Notes
1. Mary C. Elliott. "Class All the Way." *Threads* magazine, September 1989, 30.
2. Ibid.
3. Ibid.

THE ORIGINAL READY-TO-WEAR

There is a reason why, when a woman donned a Norell dress and experienced its fit, shape, and lightness, she was hooked for life and became a devoted client. Norell had never liked the look of a snug fit, preferring shapes that flattered a woman's body, skimming over the bust and the hips and, in the case of the chemise, slightly tapering. Before the French thought they invented the chemise in the 1950s, Norell's straight, 1920s-style, dropped-waist dresses were bestsellers. The designer never skimped on construction and insisted that perfect finishing was the key to keeping garments shaped and light in weight. This was unique to Norell and not a practice that other high-end designers lived by. Fabrics, weight, linings, and facings were the secret. The would-be copyists worked only from Norell's pattern and that, clearly, was not enough. Norman Norell had worked long and hard to create the exquisite construction that equaled that of the French couture—the only difference was, and it is a huge difference, his creations were ready-to-wear, not made to measure.

Right: Wool melton, side-wrapped coat with half belt and fox boa, mid-1960s. Overleaf: Norell at his desk, surrounded by fabric swatches. Photograph by Leo Friedman.

PART II: THE HISTORY

PORTRAIT OF THE DESIGNER AS A YOUNG MAN

Norman David Levinson was born on April 20, 1900, in Noblesville, Indiana, the second son of Harry and Nettie Kinsey Levinson. His mother was Methodist and his father was Jewish; the family business was a haberdashery established by his grandfather. Harry additionally opened a profitable men's hat shop in Indianapolis, where he sold cheap hats for one dollar and expensive ones for three—eventually, he wisely split the difference and priced all his hats at two dollars. The business grew and prospered, and ultimately the Levinsons moved the twenty-eight miles from Noblesville to the larger city of Indianapolis with young Norman and his older brother, Frank, who helped his father operate the store.

Weakened by rheumatic fever and recurring illnesses when he was young, Norman missed more school than not and as a result had limited opportunities to play with other children. Instead, he became devoted to his mother, Nettie, a self-avowed "nut about clothes" who, in the early 1900s, was sufficiently interested in *la mode*, subscribed to French fashion magazines, and dressed in what were thought of as extreme clothes for a Midwestern city. Her neighbors may have gossiped or gawked, but, apparently, their stares never fazed Nettie.

Norman loved to go shopping with his mother, and the two of them particularly enjoyed going to the theater on Saturday afternoons. Because his father placed advertisements for his stores in the theater's playbills, the family was entitled to three free tickets to the shows. By the time Norman was eight years old, he and his mother, and often his father or a friend, would spend Saturday afternoons at Keith's Vaudeville,

Norell as a child in his Peter Thomson sailor suit. Nautical themes would become a prevalent feature in the designer's later collections.

where he thrilled to the dazzling productions. The boy was mesmerized by the costumes, the music, the gaudiness, the razzmatazz. It was at Keith's that young Norman fell madly in love with the spangled (i.e. sequined) costumes the chorus girls wore—a passion that he would harbor throughout his life. Vaudeville was an obvious influence on Norell, who in later years remarked that the glittering stage costumes he loved as a boy were more influential on his work than anything he studied at design school.

Nettie was Norman's first model. On a train trip from Indianapolis to California in 1920, he created an ensemble for his mother worthy of notice: floor-length red chiffon dress, large straw hat bedecked with ribbons and flowers, and lace-trimmed parasol. Norell recalled that nobody spoke a word to them, the other passengers suspecting that they were gypsies.

With no serious interest in academics, Norman was not terribly keen on attending college, but he did warm to the thought of studying art in New York City. After spending a brief period at Parsons School of Design learning figure drawing and fashion illustration, he transferred to Pratt Institute and began to devote himself to his real love: costume design. According to the designer, his professors pretty much let him do as he pleased. When Norell entered a contest at Pratt and won one hundred dollars for a blouse design, he was motivated by his prize and began to spend hours and hours at the New York Public Library, where he became a fixture, poring over fashion illustrations. While still in school, dreaming of his future, Norman decided to change his surname. He was told that he needed a fancier moniker to get the theatrical work he desired, so he dropped Levinson for Norell: *Nor* from Norman, *L* from Levinson, and another *L* at the end, just for looks.

By age twenty-two, he was designing his first costumes for theatrical designer Gilbert Clark, who hired him to design all the costumes for Paramount's *A Sainted Devil* (1921), a silent movie starring the darkly handsome Rudolph Valentino. He also costumed silver screen star Gloria Swanson for *Zaza* (1923) and other films, until the studio headed west to Hollywood. The following year, he was working for Brooks Costume Company, making towering headdresses and sweeping trains and—to his enormous delight—lots of spangled creations for the chorus girls. He also made

Gloria Swanson in the 1923 silent movie *Zaza*. The actress played a French music hall temptress who, with the help of a Norell-designed wardrobe, seduces a married man.

Above and Opposite: Three
of Norell's early vaudeville
costume drawings that
show his penchant for over-
the-top glamour.

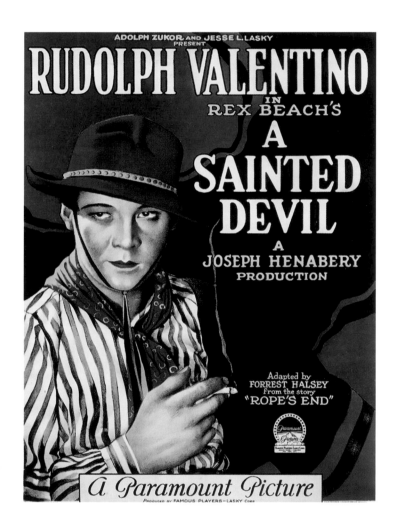

Above: A poster for the 1921 silent movie *A Sainted Devil*, for which Norell created costumes for star Rudolph Valentino. Opposite: A still from the movie, showing a costume with overblown, striped bishop's sleeves, which would soon become a leitmotif in Norell's ready-to-wear designs.

stage clothes for third-rate vaudeville and burlesque stars. It was a job Norell fondly remembered in later years. He also anonymously created costumes for the Ziegfeld Follies and earned some credits for his work at the Cotton Club.

In 1924, after three-plus years in the theater, Norell took a job with Charles Armour, a wholesale dress manufacturer in New York City, where he designed what were then considered expensive dresses, ranging from thirty-nine to one hundred dollars. After learning some basics from Armour, he was ready for new challenges.

THE HATTIE CARNEGIE YEARS

Enter Hattie Carnegie (née Kanengeiser), an entrepreneurial immigrant from Austria, who had named herself after Andrew Carnegie, who was then the richest man in America. Hattie could neither cut nor sew, but with a terrific eye and a brilliant business mind she had worked her way to the top of a multi-million-dollar fashion business with more than a thousand employees. Norell had heard through the grapevine that the head designer at Carnegie's salon, Emmet Joyce, had quit his job, so he made a beeline to Carnegie's office with some sketches, and waited all day to see her. He just sat there in the office and finally caught Carnegie's eye just as she was about to

Above: Norell and a technician, draping fabric on a dress form at Hattie Carnegie in 1939. Opposite: Striped evening ensemble (dress, belt, organza cape, and slip) by Norman Norell for Hattie Carnegie, 1932. Drawing by Michael Vollbracht.

leave for the day. Norell pleaded that if he could work for her for several weeks, he'd do it for nothing, even offering to pay for any material he ruined. And that's how he convinced Carnegie to hire him.

A formidable woman, imperious despite her four-foot-ten-inch frame, Carnegie had one of the most prestigious fashion businesses in the world: a custom operation, a retail store, and a wholesale enterprise that distributed her merchandise to stores throughout the country. The woman who freely admitted that she, herself, could not design at all, knew a great deal about style and taught Norell a good deal about elegance.

Carnegie was in the habit of sailing twice a year to Paris, where she would purchase fashions from all the top custom salons. From the late 1920s to 1940, Norell helped her choose the clothes; they would bring them back to New York and then translate them into American terms. Norell was able to examine the finest French couture garments in the world, amounting to an extraordinary education, learning the precise techniques and closely held secrets of the couturier for creating custom-made clothes. Carnegie would buy countless outfits a season so that she and Norell could pore over the construction, taking the clothes apart to see how they were made. The young designer literally pulled apart hundreds of these designs to see how they were constructed, allowing him to recognize and appreciate their quality.

Above and Opposite:
Actress Gertrude
Lawrence in a tulle chiffon
and embroidered ostrich
feathered gown, designed
by Norell for Hattie
Carnegie, for the Broadway
show *Lady in the Dark*,
1941.

Norell spent twelve years working with Carnegie, and the education he received was arguably the equivalent of attending the École de la Chambre Syndicale de la Couture Parisienne, one of the top fashion schools in Paris. Although Carnegie was difficult, she knew what she was doing, and Norell stayed with her, learning the ropes by dissecting the couture (Chanel, Patou, Vionnet), understanding and perfecting techniques, and transforming Parisian styles for the American proportion and way of life.

Stage-struck from his early childhood, Norell was thrilled to work for Carnegie, whose workshop created costumes for major stars of the theater, among them Constance Bennett, Paulette Goddard, Lilyan Tashman, Pola Negri, Joan Crawford, Katharine Hepburn, and Gertrude Lawrence. In fact, it was a dress he designed for Lawrence for the play *Lady in the Dark* that put an end to Norell's relationship with his boss. He had created a theatrical royal-blue sequined dress with an enormous skirt that was meant to be part of a dream sequence. Actress Gertrude Lawrence was delighted with her dress with its feathery ostrich plumes, and so was the audience, but Carnegie thought the costume was far too complicated and too expensive to replicate for her clients. Norell disagreed with his boss and flatly refused to simplify the dress. Turning insult into injury, Norell told his boss that she should just focus on the old lady clothes. The designer was fired on the spot. But, Lawrence's costume was a hit with the audience, and so was the show; the only problem was that Norman Norell was out of a job. Perhaps, that reality was just the catalyst he needed to soar.

By the time he left Hattie Carnegie in 1941, Norell had accumulated enough technical knowledge and dressmaking ability from studying the couture fashions of Europe that he was fully ready to bring the aura of Parisian salons to the showrooms of Seventh Avenue. And that's just what he did. Norell was the right man in the right business at the right time.

TRAINA-NORELL PARTNERSHIP

Norell wasn't jobless for long. Respected Seventh Avenue veteran Anthony Traina. who was known as a manufacturer of expensive clothes for mature women who wore large sizes, called Norell and asked him to join him as a partner in his business. Norell replied that he designed for women in smaller sizes and that is what he preferred to do. Traina agreed to produce smaller-sized clothes and offered Norell a partnership, proposing a larger salary if Norell's name was not used, or a smaller amount if it was. Norell wisely chose the lesser amount, and although he never actually owned a piece of the business, he was well aware that having his name on the label would ultimately be worth a great deal.

Traina-Norell was an ideal fit for Norell: Traina was a tough but well-respected businessman whose company focused on applying refined touches and luxurious simplicity to ready-made clothes. The American fashion industry had always depended on Paris for its ideas, but with the Second World War occupying much of Europe, its sources had dried up. European fashions were few and far between, and American designers were finally motivated to do original work. According to the *New York Times* fashion editor Bernadine Morris, "It was only then that Seventh Avenue, as it exists today, began to take form."

Norell's timing was perfect. With an education in custom-made clothes and the business of mass production, he was set. He came to fame in 1941 with his first collection for Traina, and there was no stopping him.

Unlike most of the other designers on Seventh Avenue, Norell didn't show just a line of dresses or coats. He showed a collection—a decidedly American one that

took care of the fashion needs of many women. His first collection for Traina-Norell was akin to a declaration of independence from the European designers. Norell helped make it possible for the American fashion industry to set its own direction. Finally, women would not feel it necessary to wear French labels to confirm their taste and status.

Norell was savvy enough to hire pioneer fashion publicist Eleanor Lambert to represent him. He was one of the first designers to hire a professional to help promote his clothes, and it paid off handsomely. After a year designing with Traina, with Lambert's public relations support, he received in 1943 the very first Coty Award, which became one of the most prestigious awards in fashion. In 1951, Norell was honored with his second Coty Award. He was named the first designer to be admitted to the Coty Hall of Fame and dubbed Coty's first "Immortal" designer in 1956, and was acknowledged with additional distinctions, in 1958 and 1966 for those years' collections.

For the twenty years that Norell was leading his hyphenated business life as partner in Traina-Norell, he was still polishing the technical skills that catapulted him to the top of America's fashion business. Traina-Norell was a huge success from the start: veteran fashion editor Carrie Donovan declared, "The best-made merchandise in the world was Traina-Norell." Such was the recognition of the quality of his clothes that in the movie *Sweet Smell of Success* (1957), Burt Lancaster's character says about an aspiring starlet, "The brains may be Jersey City, but the clothes are Traina-Norell!"

Above: Norell adjusting an embroidered head scarf on a model wearing a spangled coat, while another model in full, festive black skirt, patterned with bright, gilded leaves, looks on, 1943. Opposite: One of Norell's favorite coat shapes. Boxy, straight-lined jackets over short coatdresses, with matching straw shantung hats. Traina-Norell, Spring 1944. Photograph by John Rawlings.

Actress Linda Darnell in a waist-cinching corset dress by Traina-Norell, 1945. Photograph by John Rawlings.

Page 114: Traina-Norell
Roman-striped, sequined
evening sheath worn by
Dovima, 1959. Photograph
by William Helburn. Page
115: Roman-striped wool
jersey blouse, worn with
a beige wool jersey jacket
lined in the same stripes
and a matching beige wool
jersey skirt. Traina-Norell,
1944. Photograph by
John Rawlings. Opposite:
Romantic mink-hemmed
wool crepe evening gown
by Traina-Norell, 1956.

Actress Loretta Young
wears a version of the
short, formal summer
dinner dress, perfect for
an evening of hotel-roof
dancing. Orange silk
chiffon trimmed with black
lace by Traina-Norell,
Spring 1942. Photograph
by John Rawlings.

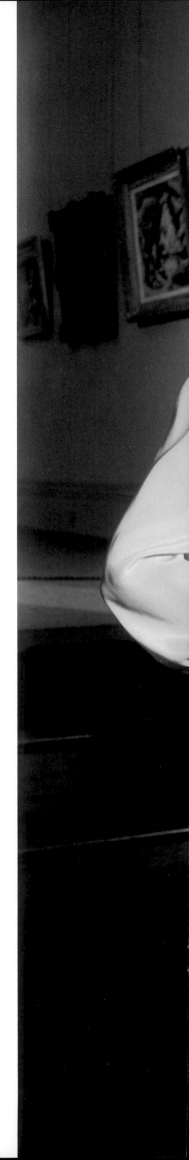

Norell borrows from the
boys with his slim, trim
sleeveless vest, neat
and professional in the
workplace, solid on the
front and patterned with
thin horizontal stripes on
the back. Traina-Norell,
early 1940s. Photograph
by Genevieve Naylor.

All that jazz. The cover of
Vogue magazine, April 1,
1949. Black-and-white
polka dots and wide-
brimmed hats in front of a
backdrop inspired by Henri
Matisse's sensational mural
Jazz. Photograph by
Cecil Beaton.

Under the umbrella, a
veiled hat, creamy pearls,
and a Traina-Norell
pilgrim-collared linen
coatdress, Spring 1950.
Photograph by Erwin
Blumenfeld.

VOGUE

PARIS
COLLECTIONS
2ND REPORT

*American
Spring Fashions
à la carte*

GIVE +

Incorporating Vanity Fair
March 15, 1950
Price 50 Cents
in U. S. and Canada
$1.00 All Other Countries

Above: Divine moiré ball
gown with deep mink
cuffs at the elbow, Fall
1957. Photograph by
John Rawlings. Opposite:
Flowered blouson silk
crepe dress with a bateau
neck, Spring 1958.
Photograph by Irving Penn.

Opposite: Despite wartime
fabric restrictions, Norell
managed to make clothes
that were smart and
sophisticated. Lavender
silk-crepe shirtdress
with matching umbrella,
Spring 1944. Photograph
by John Rawlings. Page
130: Lovely as a summer's
eve. Norell's pink cotton
organdy bodice and skirt
appliquéd with white flowers, Traina-Norell, Spring
1954. Drawing by Carl
Oscar August Erickson.
Page 131: Everything's
coming up roses in a pretty,
sleeveless, aquamarine and
ivory striped, full-skirted
dance dress, strewn with
rose petals, Spring 1953.
Photograph by Erwin
Blumenfeld.

Cropped blouson jacket of
ruby-colored wool jersey
over a navy blue wool
skirt and white silk shirt.
Traina-Norell, Fall 1954.
Photograph by Erwin
Blumenfeld.

Above: Jean Patchett in
Traina-Norell's tweed
flyaway bolero jacket
and slim sheath, 1957.
Photograph by John
Rawlings. Opposite: A
dramatic evening look.
Cranberry crepe peplum
with back-crossed straps
and tiered skirt to the floor,
Fall 1955. Photograph by
Karen Radkai.

Above: Norell was one of
the first designers to appreciate the luxury and beauty
of leopard—both real
and faux. Here, a Traina-
Norell leopard coat, 1943.
Photograph by Louise
Dahl-Wolfe. Opposite:
Traina-Norell's mid-calf
dresses in patterns of
python and leopard, Spring
1947. Photograph by
Serge Balkin.

Sheelagh Gordon-Manno
in a black silk faille dress
embroidered with a
magnificent bouquet of
flowers on its rounded
skirt, Spring 1964.

HIS OWN LABEL

By the time Traina retired in 1959, Norell was more than ready to assume ownership of the company. With the support of two out-of-town investors, the designer opened his own firm, Norman Norell, Inc., at prestigious 550 Seventh Avenue, where most of the elite American designers had their showrooms. Norell owned 51 percent of the stock and complete creative freedom. Now, instead of the ladies referring to their clothes as their "Trainas" they could speak reverently of their "Norells." Some went so far as to label their Norells the "Rolls-Royces" of the fashion industry.

For his first collection under his own name, Norell wanted change, even controversy, so he proposed something quite provocative. The designer owned an arresting portrait of the Marchesa Luisa Casati walking along a canal in Venice, in a chemise dress, with short hair, ultra-white skin, and smudged eyes encircled with burnt black cork (see pages 170–71). The painting, by artist Kees van Dongen, was Norell's pride and joy, and the remarkable lady it portrayed served as muse for his first show of the 1960s, which was inspired by the 1920s. Yvonne Presser, one of Norell's models, had recently been to Paris with the designer where she spied a waiter with a stylish haircut, reminiscent of the short, cropped hair of the flappers of the '20s. She found out who cut his hair and immediately went to the waiter's barber to get the identical cut. When she got back to New York and showed it off, it became quite the rage.

In June 1960, Norell presented his collection with a nod to van Dongen, and Presser and her fellow models all wore white and green makeup, kohl-rimmed eyes, and shingled haircuts, looking like '60s versions of '20s flappers, with all the insouciance to match. "The attitude of those girls with those clothes—the audience was spellbound," said Lynn Manulis, daughter of Martha Phillips, whose boutique, Martha, always sold closetfuls of Norell designs. "Norell was thrilled," Presser added. "It was as though it were the first time he'd been set free from a cage."

The exotic, white-faced, smudge-eyed, short-haired look was not the only hit at the show, but as a sidebar it prompted three beauty trends and sent prices for van Dongen's art through the roof. It also presented some cutting-edge ideas.

Norell had an uncanny instinct for anticipating change. His collection for Fall 1960 introduced divided skirts, or culottes, to make life easier for women to wear in the city, "climbing in and out of taxis, traveling, walking." The designer was so confident about his new design that he offered the pattern for his culottes to any manufacturer in the world who wanted it at no cost, in order to avoid inferior interpretations. Afraid that shoddy imitations of his culottes would endanger public acceptance of his style, but willing to have them imitated if they were done properly, he had the specifications published in *Women's Wear Daily*, soon after his Spring 1962 collection was presented. The culottes started the biggest wave of piracy in the garment industry. Five French couturiers borrowed the culottes two years after Norell had introduced them.

Norell debuted his culottes walking suit, which paired pleated, cropped pants with a tailored jacket. It was his early version of the trouser-turnout that a few years later would give birth to the classic pantsuit: a safari-type jacket and straight pants. (Yves Saint Laurent was often mentioned as the originator of the ladies' pantsuit, but Norell was there a full year before.) The audience's reaction to the master's first show of the 1960s was shock and awe, and the standing ovation at the end was both loud and long.

Clockwise, from top left: Norell with model Dorine McKay in Italy; the designer with Revlon's Paul Woolard, left, and Max Bernegger, right, on Seventh Avenue in New York City; Norell at the Bridge of Sighs, Venice; Norell with Bernegger, Venice. All photographs from the mid-1960s.

Norell had hit the ground running. The timing was perfect; the advent of the '60s brought with it a new, more avant-garde experimentation, within the confines of classic American style tempered by the highest quality workmanship to be found anywhere in the ready-to-wear industry.

When Norell wasn't working, which was almost never, he was apt to be dining with his pals at his favorite eateries. Hamburger Heaven was one of his haunts: when he entered the restaurant, the waiters would supply him with a stack of white paper napkins so he could start sketching his ideas before he was served. Schrafft's, the popular restaurant on 43rd Street, east of Broadway and close to his 550 Seventh Avenue workrooms, was his choice at lunch. According to the *New York Times*'s Bernadine Morris, it was because of Norell that this particular Schrafft's had become "the place to be": the garment center's answer to the Algonquin's Round Table, but filled with colorful designers rather than writers. No booze-fueled, three-hour lunches took place when Norell was there: fastidious Norell stuck to a tight schedule, meals never exceeded an hour, and almost no one exceeded one drink. There was, however, a great deal of lively conversation among the mix of mostly Seventh Avenue friends, among them Wilson Folmar, Bobby Knox, Alan Graham, Louis Clausen, Frank Adams, and John Moore.

John Moore and dress manufacturer Mattie Talmack in the Dior–New York showroom, 1954. Moore, a designer in his own right, was Norell's intimate friend for over twenty years. Photograph by Mark Shaw.

ON HIS OWN: NORELL GROWS HIS BUSINESS

A fter years of working for others, Norell had finally established his own company under his own label, and his popularity had begun to soar. His first collection, which debuted in June 1960, was both brilliant and daring *and* indicated a new Norell taking charge. As the seasons went on, the designer's name accrued tremendous status and more and more women were clamoring to buy his clothes. But there was a hitch: because his designs were considered so desirable, there was a lot of copying. The minute one of his dresses went down the runway, a photograph would be taken, and in a wink, a pseudo-Norell dress would be created. Norell realized he needed outside help and, when he was in Europe buying fabric in 1963, had the good fortune to hire a savvy, young Swiss textile salesman to head his United States production team. Dynamic and brimming with ideas, Max Bernegger was able to vastly increase Norell's business.

A year and a half after Bernegger joined Norell in New York, the December 21, 1964, issue of *Women's Wear Daily*, never missing a beat, explained the business behind the glamour. Jean Weir reported:

Since Swiss Max joined Indiana's Norell just 18 months ago, business is booming.

Not only were 1,200 more pieces shipped this year, but 65 to 70 per cent more coats and suits were shipped.

Not a single person was added to Norell's production set-up, yet there's been a gigantic increase in the number of working hours.

Gone are the days when Norell's back room closed down for two to three months. "Now they come begging for a vacation," says Max.

Taking time out from his spring fittings, Norman talks about his fall successes: "We showed 173 styles—how in the hell it got that big I don't know—but out of that fall collection (or any line, for that matter)

Norell's soft feminine shirtwaist in heathered-oatmeal wool jersey, with a row of buttons, wide belt, and a big taffeta bow, late 1960s.

we never have a discard. Even if we only get an order for one—we'll make it. Other houses will discard a style if they get less than 10. But I feel we owe it to our customers to make what they've ordered.

"Our jersey dresses are always good. Some people think jersey is easy to do—but I believe it's one of the most difficult fabrics to handle. I have just one patternmaker to whom I will give my jerseys, he understands them. Even though our jerseys are expensive, we have no competition on them."

When is a Norell a big success? Just how many of a style have to be sold before Norman and Max considers it a Hit? Well, it breaks down something in this way:

- 350 pieces of each daytime jersey style
- 75–100 pieces of each three-piece wool costume
- 75 pieces per color of each belted coat
- 100 pieces of each black wool dress
- 10–20 of each floor-length beaded dress at $1,600 to $1,700 a style.

There's lots of behind-the-scenes know-how that puts the Norman Norell label across. As Max Bernegger admits, "Mr. Norell is one of the most astute businessmen ... he's too shy to say so ... but I know this side of him." There is terrific coordination between Norell's design room and Bernegger's business office. They also have the courage and knowledge of knowing what's going to be good. "We cut stock ahead of our show," explains Max. "Just as soon as Mr. Norell is through with a sample we start duplicating and cutting ahead. This way, although we show late—we ship early."

The strategic timing was successful in reducing the amount of pseudo-Norells: in showing late, a month and a half after others, copies weren't being made from photographs of the collection. Producing early and getting clothes into stores quashed the demand for copies. Bernegger explained, "Business was increased enormously: over a million dollars the first year. We took the risk away. This was all based on the first year because of early production. It was very profitable. The women who bought early were very happy to show off before their friends had the clothes. I Magnin, Bergdorf, Saks—they already had customers, but they were extremely happy when they got the orders early. It turned out really well."

Everything was produced at 550 Seventh Avenue, except the jersey dresses, which were made in New Jersey. "We always had a line of jersey dresses—I cut hundreds of them—and amazingly, we got re-orders two and three weeks after the delivery," Bernegger said. Bernegger worked for Norell from 1963 to 1969, working alongside about one hundred draftsmen and tailors. "We had a great relationship and mutual respect, which is more important than anything else. Quality always lasts, and if you pay a high price, you certainly want it to last. Norman Norell was so demanding when it came to quality, you could not move him an inch. It had to be perfect!"

For twenty years up to this time, Norell shared a close relationship with John Moore, though they never lived together. Norell had met the handsome, talented young Moore when the latter was a student at Parsons. Moore started out working for several Seventh Avenue designers and, finally in 1963 with financial help from Norell, he started his own business. For a while, Moore had his share of successes, especially when he was chosen to design Lady Bird Johnson's yellow satin inaugural dress and matching sable-trimmed coat in 1964 (Moore was a Texan, like the Johnsons). He had received a coveted Coty Award in 1953 for his evening dresses when working for Mattie Talmack, but to Norell's great disappointment, Moore never received the recognition his friend had hoped he would achieve: his unfortunate penchant for heavy drinking had seriously gotten in his way. Norell could fund him for only so long, and Moore ended up having to shutter his business in 1970. Ultimately, Moore left New York to head back home to Alice, Texas, where he put his design talents to use, making costumes for the local high school plays, crafting beautiful picture frames, and helping run his family's antiques business.

Norell, the man who lent enormous cachet to an industry that was still called the "rag business," was turning out his trademark simple but elegant clothes at a faster pace than ever. At the end of a day, when Norell had finished choosing fabrics, sketching, designing, pinning, supervising production, and changing the width of a jacket shoulder by an eighth of an inch, he would finally escape the din of Seventh Avenue and head for home. There, in the light-filled drawing room of his Amster Yard duplex, he was surrounded by the elegant objects of past centuries that he had so carefully collected. A devotee of auction houses, both in Paris and New York, eagle-eyed Norell had filled his home with rare and beautiful things: a gorgeous antique lacquered Coromandel screen, Baccarat crystal chandeliers, fine Aubusson rugs, and ancient Chinese porcelains. His taste in fabrics and home furnishings was as elegant as the cut of his widely admired dresses. As much as he lived for the chaos and the fulfillment of his workday, he loved just being at home.

Norell's slinky silver-
sequined pajamas,
photographed at Norell's
New York apartment,
1966. Photograph by
Horst P. Horst.

A BRAND IS BORN

Norell had reached the fashion summit: no one else in America had the prestige, the cult following, or the clout that he possessed. In rapid-fire succession, Norell designed some elegant mid-heel shoes for Belgian Shoes in New York and also designed gorgeous scarves from Italy in luxurious Abraham silk twill. Bernegger—who was a friend of Zurich-based Abraham's founder, Gustav Zumsteg—arranged for Norell to work closely with Zumsteg to create a line of gorgeous heavy twill silk oblong and square signature scarves, printed in Zurich and finished in Italy.

But the biggest license was yet to come: as the story goes, when Charles Revson, the founder and chairman of Revlon cosmetics, asked his lissome wife, Lyn, an avid collector of Norell dresses, what she would like for Christmas, she answered immediately that she wanted a perfume for Norman. It was a brilliant idea: there wasn't a single American fashion designer who had his or her own fragrance.

Bernegger contacted Charles Revson and, along with Revlon vice president Paul Woolard, took part in the creation of a sophisticated American fragrance. The result was one of the most successful American perfume launches ever and one of the best-known, best-loved scents in the United States. Bottled in a beautifully beveled, cut-crystal flacon and housed in a chic white box with an elegantly elongated Norell logo in black, and just below it, in fine lettering, New York—the package telegraphed the impeccable taste and classic simplicity of its namesake designer.

The fragrance was launched in 1968 and was lauded as an immediate success throughout the United States. It allowed the sixty-eight-year-old Norell to buy out the investors in his company and become financially whole for the first time in his life.

Norell perfume, created for Revlon, 1968.

Above: Norman Norell
displaying two of his
shoe designs as part of a
collaboration with Belgian
Shoes, owned by Henri
Bendel, 1967. Opposite:
Stars-and-stripes scarf,
part of a series created by
Norell for Gustav Zumsteg
of the fabled Swiss mill
Abraham, 1969.

JUNE 1969   # BAZAAR   HARPERS   75¢

THINGS
TO BE
HAPPY
ABOUT:

NEW
SHAPES IN
SHIRTS

NEW
JEWELS FOR
THE BODY

NEW
SECRETS
OF
BEAUTY

THE
BEST-DRESSED
YACHTS
BY EUGENIA
SHEPPARD

Above: Norell's celadon
reefer coatdress, narrowly
belted in white leather
with a luxe, white silk scarf,
Spring 1967. Photograph
by Irving Penn. Opposite:
Norell's sunshine-yellow
narrow double-breasted
coatdress belted in black
patent leather, Spring 1967.
Photograph by Irving Penn.

Ladies who lunch. Norell's
lavish fox-trimmed turn-
outs: a dress with a narrow
bolero jacket in beige
wool twill and a cropped
jacket with dirndl skirt in
red-and-black tweed plaid,
Fall 1967.

Above: Agnona baby
alpaca gingham swing coat
in beige and white with
large bone buttons from
Norell's last collection,
Fall 1972. Opposite: The
same swing coat, worn
by Samantha Jones,
over a matching alpaca
gauze gingham high-
necked dress. Photograph
by Bob Stone.

158

Opposite: Drawing of
Norell's throat-latched
capelet suit with jersey
shell top, 1964. Above:
Suit composed of a
double-breasted wool
capelet over a matching
sleeveless dress worn
with a narrow patent
leather belt, 1964.

Gorgeous warp-printed
floral taffeta dress to the
floor with billowing sleeves
and a beautifully bowed
back, 1963.

Lauren Hutton in Norell's fine-feathered coat and chocolate-brown sequined turtleneck sheath dress, Fall 1971. Photograph by Bert Stern.

Above: Norell's Oxford
wool suit — shaped jacket,
bow at the neck, and a skirt
with inverted pleats, 1964.
Drawing by Kenneth Paul
Block. Opposite: Olive wool
twill suit with passemen-
terie trim, early 1960s.
Overleaf: Norell's black
dolman-sleeved gown,
covered with bugle beads
on silk chiffon, 1972.

HONORING A LEGEND

There was really no one who could compare to Norell. His take on designing fashion never changed radically: it was clearly a logical progression—adding, subtracting, refining, and seeking perfection all the way. Case in point: leagues of Norell-wearing women could count on visiting their closets and selecting a dress they might have worn ten or fifteen years before, knowing that it would be the perfect choice for that night. Norell was quality—American quality—all the way.

The simple, elegant shapes, the extraordinary fabrics, and the flattering fit were all exceptional. The designer's preoccupation with detail, both on the inside and outside of a dress or suit, gave it a perfect line. The "inside knowledge" (literally) that Norell had accumulated over his long fifty-year design career had impacted every inch of his work.

By the early 1970s, Norell had achieved enormous success, collected countless awards, and received accolades. Ann Keagy—chairwoman of the Fashion Design Department at Parsons School of Design, where Norell had taught for twenty years— decided to mount a Norell retrospective that would reflect his extraordinary body of work from the 1930s to 1970, selecting from over one thousand mint-condition pieces for the show, sourced from Norell's clients all over the country. Sadly, the day before the show was to open at the Metropolitan Museum of Art in New York City, Norell suffered a cerebral hemorrhage and passed away ten days later, never seeing his own exhibition for himself.

The next event to celebrate Norell's life and considerable talent was his funeral on October 27, 1972. The designer would have loved the service at Unitarian Church of All Souls on Lexington Avenue in New York: Bobby Short playing Cole Porter, Noel Coward, and the love song "My Ship" from *Lady in the Dark*. One of Norell's favorites, the song's lyrics begin, "My ship has sails that are made of silk." The Reverend Walter Donald Kring read Psalm 121 and a selection of poetry by Rabindranath Tagore. Dr. Kevin Cahill, Norell's physician, delivered a eulogy, and Charles Revson called his departure "a tragedy to the fashion world and to the city where fashion is king." Mrs. John V. Lindsay, wife of the city's mayor, acknowledged the loss of two great men of the city: baseball legend Jackie Robinson was being mourned at a funeral on the same day.

The most meaningful comment came from Carmello Cardello, Norell's head tailor for many years: "You didn't have to put a label on them; people recognized his clothes."

Pages 170–71: Norell's models in every iteration of his famous hand-sewn sequined mermaid gowns, Fall 1960. Photograph by Milton H. Greene. Opposite: Norell, looking like the country squire, in his New York apartment with its light-hearted slipcovers and draperies for summer, 1969. Photograph by Francesco Scavullo.

PART III: THE LEADING LADIES

A s one of America's most highly regarded designers, Norell worked with a number of glamorous theater and movie actresses, television personalities, society swans, and others who were looking for clothes that had the singular elegance and star quality that only he could provide.

In November 1960, just after her husband was elected President, Jacqueline Bouvier Kennedy allowed a *Women's Wear Daily* (*WWD*) illustrator to sketch two Norell cocktail dresses that she had chosen to wear in the White House once she and the President took up residence in January 1961. The dresses were both understated Norell and classic Jackie: a superbly simple black wool dress with a gently dropped waistline and a fine purple wool over-blouse and narrow skirt. The caption above the sketches in *WWD* reads: "Jacqueline Elects Norell!"

The divinely elegant Babe Paley, née Barbara Cushing, was one of three beautiful sisters from Boston. With her tall frame and regal bearing, she looked as though she was custom made for Norell's simple and precise dresses. Norell adored her because she was as nice as she was chic and lovely. And the international socialite, fashion icon, and world-class beauty Gloria Guinness—a lady very friendly with Balenciaga, Dior, and Saint Laurent, and who loved Valentino and Givenchy—was simply mad about Norell.

Marilyn Monroe chose a dazzling Norell dress to wear on the evening she was to receive the Golden Globe Henrietta Award for World Film Favorites in 1962. It was a gorgeous, deep emerald-green, jersey floor-length mermaid gown, covered with sparkling green sequins. But when Marilyn appeared to receive her award, the halter-neck

Lauren Bacall in Norell's silk crepe low-torso scarf dress with rhinestone-buckled belt, 1966. Photograph by Jack Mitchell.

Babe Mortimer (later Babe
Paley) in Traina-Norell
color-blocked blue and
black wool, 1946. Norell
adored Babe, a *Vogue*
fashion editor and an
aristocratic beauty with
unflaggingly good taste
and manners. Photograph
by Horst P. Horst.

dress had sequined straps hanging from both shoulders. She must have known that her arms were meant to go through those straps. It appeared that Marilyn had lost a little weight and her bust had lost a bit of its bulk. Apparently, she had worried that if she wore the dress as designed, it might flatten her—and a flattened chest was one thing Marilyn would not stand for, even with a Golden Globe in her hand.

Norell also designed Monroe's dress for her wedding to playwright Arthur Miller in June 1956. The ceremony took place in Roxbury, Connecticut, at Miller's country house. Norell and John Moore, his partner, collaborated on the dress, with Norman creating the design and John doing the draping. The dress was a mid-length, body-skimming sheath with an empire waist and a ruched bust, which accentuated Marilyn's curves.

Television personality and entertainer Dinah Shore couldn't live without Norell's gorgeous gowns. As soon as his new line would come into the stores, her *vendeuse* would call her and set up an appointment. Shore always said that her working clothes were always by Norell because they stood up better than anyone else's. She estimated that she had performed in one sequined dress 150 times in the previous year. And, she commented that the dress was as good as the day she bought it.

After the willowy and glamorous actress Lauren Bacall discovered Norell, she rarely strayed from him for her personal wardrobe. Bacall also had the privilege of wearing Norell in the movie *Sex and the Single Girl* (1964). With her perfect model's body and sultry looks, she was truly stunning in Norell's gold, silver, and copper pailleted mermaid dresses, which she wore for more than thirty years. "Almost everything

Above: Marilyn Monroe received a Golden Globe Henrietta Award for World Film Favorites in 1962, wearing a dazzling emerald-green mermaid gown. Photograph by Michael Ochs. Opposite: Lauren Bacall, in beaded silk crepe, kicking up a leg, while being fitted by Norell himself, 1966. Photograph by Tony Palmieri.

Above: Singer, actress, and
television personality Dinah
Shore in Norell's mid-length
bolero jacket suit, 1970.
Opposite: Shore modeling
two looks by Norell. One is
a full-feathered evening
coat, which was featured on
the cover of the September
26, 1960, issue of *Life*
magazine. The other outfit
includes a sleeveless
cocktail dress with a softly
pleated skirt and beaded
bodice, worn with a
matching scarf.

I have is from him," said Bacall in the May 16, 1966, issue of *Women's Wear Daily*. "When I lived in Paris I had everything from Givenchy and Chanel—but Norman is as good as anything in Paris. He and Chanel make equally comfortable clothes—what more do you need? Norman's are trimmer—and I like them."

Lyn Revson, the wife of Charles Revson of Revlon cosmetics fame, was another die-hard fan of Norell's who adored his clothes, particularly his sequined gowns, in which she was photographed for *Vogue* magazine. Her mother presented her with her first Norell on her eighteenth birthday—a slinky black dress with crisscrossing straps in back. Her admiring husband Charles loved the way she looked in Norell's glittering sequined mermaid gowns, which she collected in a range of shimmering rainbow shades.

Doris Day wore wonderful Norell outfits in the charmingly comedic movie *That Touch of Mink* (1962). One day, she went to Norell's studio to look at some of his designs and brought her co-star, Cary Grant, along. Grant was so enamored of Norell's clothes and the way Day looked in them that he insisted on choosing her wardrobe for the movie; his choices were enthusiastically appreciated by all.

In the 1971 movie *Klute*, leggy and model-thin actress Jane Fonda, playing the role of a call girl, wore a form-fitting sequined blue Norell mermaid dress in a scene with Donald Sutherland in which the sexy, extra-long zipper down the back of the dress provided a provocative moment.

Smart and sassy, Lee Remick wore Norell's clothes in *The Wheeler Dealers* (1963), in which she plays a stock analyst in a fast-moving film with lots of repartee. But the real stars of the movie are Norman Norell's clothes: in offbeat colors such as olive,

Above: In the movie *Klute* (1971), Jane Fonda plays the role of a high-class call girl who, in a steamy scene, seductively removes her dark blue sequined mermaid dress, while Donald Sutherland's character waits and waits. Opposite: Norell designed a wardrobe exclusively for Lee Remick for her role as a smart and sexy business-woman in *The Wheeler Dealers* (1963). The wardrobe of simple, subtly colored clothes suited her perfectly.

caramel, pink, and saffron, and sometimes touches of black for contrast, Remick is chic, cool, and feminine in the designer's beautifully cut sleeveless dresses and neatly tailored, business-like—but not too-business-like—suits.

Marjorie Fisher, the dynamic and philanthropic wife of Detroit industrialist Max M. Fisher, adored her first Norell—a crisp white linen sailor dress with a navy bow. A long-standing fan of the designer, she freely admitted that his clothes had made up the major part of her wardrobe for years. "I think he is a genius," she said. "There is no need to look elsewhere—he makes everything from pajamas to day dresses.... I never have to shop anymore." When the designer presented his first collection of his own in 1960, Fisher adopted the same '20s "Cambridge cut" that the models sported on the runway: short, cropped, and shingled hair, which gave all of them a fresh, insouciant air. *Life* magazine was crazy about the look and photographed pages of Norell's models in the '20s-influenced clothes that he had shown that season.

"My mother simply adored Norman Norell." Fisher's daughter Mary recalls. "She considered him one of her closest friends and loved wearing all of his clothes. I remember going up to his showroom with her and seeing all those tall, lithe models wearing his samples. Then Norman would have my mother, who was tiny, try on the samples and watch as he deftly fitted the clothes to accentuate her diminutive frame.... My mother loved to laugh, and there was always laughter between her and Norell. He was always a perfect gentleman, and my mother was never quite the same after his death. My sister Marjorie and I sometimes got to wear her hand-me-down Norells, which were always in pristine condition."

The McGuire Sisters, a trio of sibling-singers with beautiful harmonizing voices, were hugely popular in the 1950s and '60s, and they were devoted to Norell. The designer frequently dressed the girls—Dorothy, Christine, and Phyllis—in sparkling paillettes and always made everything in triplicate. The sisters were said to have kept their Norells in a special vault that occupied the entire basement floor of one of their houses.

Precious Williams, a tall, blonde Memphis belle, had two great loves: her husband, Jack, and the clothes of her favorite designer, Norell. On their first date, Jack took Precious to a football game, wearing a dark green corduroy sports coat and an orange shirt. Precious was all glammed up in a red Hattie Carnegie knit dress, a sable scarf, and diamond earrings. Jack was convinced his elegant date would never go out with him again. But somehow he got the message and headed to the most sophisticated boutique in town, where he snapped up some beautiful vintage clothes for Precious, with a special eye toward the Norells. Over several decades, they amassed over a thousand vintage garments, storing them in every closet, with the overflow in their pool house. Theirs was truly a marriage with a passion for fashion.

Above, left: Ava Gardner in Norell's sequined mermaid dress with white fox stole as she arrives at the West Coast premiere of *The Barefoot Contessa* (1954) in which she starred.
Above, right: The McGuire Sisters—Christine, Dorothy, and Phyllis—in color-blocked sequins on "The Hollywood Palace" television show, mid-1960s.

Above, left: Cary Grant and Doris Day in the movie *That Touch of Mink* (1962). All of Day's clothes in the film are by Norman Norell and were chosen by Grant. Above, right: Michelle Obama wearing vintage 1950s Norell at the "Christmas in Washington" concert in 2010. Left: Carol Channing in Norell black tie at the Norell retrospective at New York's Metropolitan Museum of Art, 1972.

Norell's dramatic dolman
sleeve, bugle-beaced chiffon gown, Spring 1972.
Cher. Los Angeles. January
23, 1972. Photograph by
Richard Avedon.

Above: Lyn Revson with her favorite designer, and friend, Norman Norell, 1972. Photograph by Sal Traina. Opposite: Barbra Streisand (with her dog Sadie) on her television special "Color Me Barbra," wearing a Norell sequined jumpsuit, 1966.

Norell's empire-waisted,
side-buttoned stunner in
black wool crepe.
Judy Garland, New
York, January 7, 1963.
Photograph by Richard
Avedon.

THE ULTIMATE DESIGNER

BY DENISE LINDEN

I had always dreamed of working for Mr. Norell. One day out of the blue, Dorine McKay, Norell's favorite model, telephoned me and said Norell would like to see me. When I arrived, he graciously stood up to greet me. He singled out a dress for me to try and I went into the models' room and carefully put it on. I must say it fit me well. "Oh, that will be fine," said the master. "What size shoe do you wear? Are you available for a fitting tomorrow?" I flew out of there, insanely happy.

Norell was highly professional. His employees wore white coats in the workroom, and everything was very clean. I could tell that Mr. Norell (I never called him anything else) was of a different stripe from most other designers. "Would you be kind enough to try on this dress?" he said, in his most gentlemanly manner. When I put on the dress, I almost swooned: it was perfect in every way.

I had never been to Europe and Mr. Norell invited me to go with him to France. We stayed at the Hotel Ritz, which was unbelievably grand. This was 1968. Norell took me everywhere: Maxim's, Taillevent, Crocodile. A restaurant outside Paris filled with flowers as if it were a garden. We spent time looking at Racine's pure wool and silk jersey for Norell's trademark dresses. The material was amazing: when someone put it on, it just flowed over the body. Norell said, "We have to find a paillette man." He had a piece of camel-colored fabric in his hand. The salesman pulled out a cellophane sheet, covered with a rainbow of sequins. Norell's eye quickly found one to match his fabric. Norell was so exacting, he insisted on telling the sewer exactly where to position each flower. Then the coats would be shipped back to us in New York. When they arrived at our office, Norell was at home, sick. He instructed me to open the package, saying, "I hope they didn't put too much green in there." His premonition had been correct: they had added a green undertone to the sequins. "Ok, send it back and let him know that nothing escapes me!" He was firm, but he never got angry.

In 1962, Norell developed a cancerous vocal cord that had to be removed. Norell's doctor was somehow able to create a makeshift additional vocal cord which functioned pretty well. Norell's voice was forever hoarse and raspy after that, but once you listened to him for a while you got used to it. Since the throat surgery was just before the showing of his collection, the designer carefully screened fashion reporters and store executives. Two sessions were held later for buyers to place orders. No one was to know that he had been sick. Norman Norell was a private man and an extraordinarily courageous person.

It was an enormous pleasure to be part of the Norell *cabine*, to assist him with his business and his travels, and to learn something from him every day. I was incredibly lucky. There will never be another like him.

Above: Denise Linden modeling in a Norell show, Fall 1970. Opposite, top left: Models Dorine McKay, Claudia Halley, and Claire Eggelston, in their spangles, 1960. Photograph by Milton H. Greene. Opposite, top right: Norell with members of his *cabine*, Audrey Seder, Linden, and Deborah Burns, in the early 1970s. Opposite, bottom: Norell with models Linden and Pat Mori at a Norell trunk show at Bonwit Teller, 1972.

PART IV: THE LEGACY

THE RETROSPECTIVE: HONORING A CAREER

Ann Keagy, chairwoman of the Fashion Design Department at Parsons School of Design, adored Norell and, aware that he was considering retirement, wanted to honor him for the many extraordinary things he had done for the school and its students. She decided on the idea of mounting a Norell retrospective, covering the years from the 1930s to the early 1970s: almost a half century of designing some of the most beautiful and beautifully made women's clothes ever seen.

Keagy asked Norell to provide her with a list of some of his best customers around the country and, after contacting them about the retrospective, she set out to visit them individually and view the Norell treasures that they had amassed. Trips to Indiana, Texas, Kansas, Illinois, Michigan, California, Florida, Missouri, Massachusetts, and New York ensued, yielding choice clothes from the designer, some of them dating back to the 1930s. In the end, she had gathered more than one thousand pieces—all of them in mint condition!

Delighted with the reception she had from Norell's ladies, Keagy noted that the clothes were usually packed in trunks, beautifully wrapped in tissue paper, and treated like sacred objects. The women who had worn them always had wonderful stories about the "lives" of his creations: where they had traveled, how they had been received. Norell's clothes were perceived as cherished friends. And Norell, himself, insisted on bringing all of the accessories he had from the 1930s, '40s, and '50s that had originally been shown with the clothes, ensuring that the bags and shoes would be worn with clothes of the same vintage.

Norell suffered a stroke the day before the Metropolitan Museum of Arts's retrospective opened in his honor and never had a chance to see it: he died ten days later.

The New York Times, October 15, 1972

At Retrospective, Hundreds Applaud an Ailing Norell

By Bernadine Morris

The bravos resounded off the rafters at the Metropolitan Museum of Art last night as the stage filled with dozens of gleaming sequined dresses in every shade from silver to dark green. A radiating mass of lights, the dresses formed the finale of the first retrospective showing of fashions by Norman Norell, a designer for 50 years.

The designer wasn't there to hear the thundering applause, however. He was in the intensive care unit at Lenox Hill Hospital, having suffered a stroke on Sunday morning.

The word had gotten around Seventh Avenue that he was ill, but nobody was talking about it much as 750 men and women in evening clothes filed into the Grace Rainey Rogers auditorium. But then Dr. John Everett brought everything into the open by announcing that "Norman Norell, a frail man who worked at a frantic pace," had fallen ill. Dr. Everett is president of the New School and the Parsons School of Design.

News Shocks Many

Parsons had organized the show. Dr. Everett went on to tell the audience Norell had indicated he wanted all the festivities to go on as usual.

Many of Norell's fans, who had lent their clothes for the performance, had flown in from such places as Michigan, Texas and Florida to be present. Not having heard any of the rumors during the day on Seventh Avenue, they were the most shocked by the announcement.

"I am simply numb," said Mrs. Joseph Quay of Bloomfield Hills, Mich. "I thought the show was the most smashing one I had ever seen," said Mrs. Jay Pritzker of Winnetka, Illinois. "It's such a shame that Mr. Norell couldn't be here to see it, too."

Among the women who wore their Norells to honor the designer were Mrs. Alfred Taubman of Detroit and her friend, Mrs. Morris Lomaskin in a gold and silver sequin style.

"Wonderful Tribute"

"I was just saying to my husband what a wonderful tribute this was to happen when he was still alive," Mrs. Lomaskin said. "And now this blow ..."

Halston called it "a wonderful evening—and the saddest," and Victor Costa, the designer for Suzy Perette, looked over the audience and said, "The crowd is so beautifully dressed, Mr. Norell would have loved to see them."

Chester Weinberg said, "It was a mind-blowing experience—we all grew up with our eye on Norell. He was the father of us all."

Other designers in the audience included Donald Brooks, Dominic Rompollo, Pauline Trigere and Chuck Howard.

In addition to the sequin dresses, the show picked up other styles he had made famous: sailor dresses, which he showed recurrently throughout his career; shirtwaist dresses for day and evening with enormously full skirts, propped up by petticoats and hoops; suits with waist-length jackets and wildly flaring skirts, and sexy black dresses with deeply cut necklines and draped skirts.

Some of the women who had lent their clothes consented to model them.

Among them were Mrs. Mortimer Solomon, wife of a real estate man in Purchase, New York. She still wears the strapless evening dress with black fox on the skirt that she bought in 1953.

"Whenever I don't know what to put on, I pick this," she said, just before the show.

Mrs. Sidney Goodman flew in from Minneapolis to model, among other styles, an archetypical double-breasted Norell coat that was four years old but looked new.

"He's as good as any French designer," said Mrs. Goodman, whose husband is in real estate.

Mrs. Charles Revson, wife of the head of Revlon, which launched the perfume called "Norell" four years ago, modeled half a dozen styles, including a number of the sequin sheaths that the designer has made famous over the years.

The show started with some styles from his current collection and then followed Norell's career by decades from the 1930s on. The oldest dress in the collection is from Mrs. Barney Goodman of Kansas City, Mo. It dates back to 1932 when Mr. Norell was working for Hattie Carnegie, the Bergdorf Goodman of her day.

"That's my dress," said Mrs. Barney Goodman, when the pink and white striped dress with the ruffled capelet appeared. "He fitted me himself."

One of Their Own

The second style, a white lace design, was also here, she excitedly told her daughter, Mrs. Eugene Strauss, who was sitting next to her in a red Norell. "And that's mine, too," she went on as an evening dress with a black sweater top and a plaided sequin skirt appeared. They were both from the 1930s. "A little ahead of everyone he was with that evening sweater," she said happily.

Seventh Avenue luminaries supported the show enthusiastically, because by honoring Mr. Norell, they were honoring one of their own.

"He's the American Balenciaga," said Jerry Silverman, who took 25 tickets at $25 each so his entire staff could have "the once-in-a-lifetime opportunity" to see Norell clothes throughout the years. "He's the outstanding designer in the century," Mr. Silverman added.

The grand finale of models in sparkling mermaid gowns at the Norell retrospective in the Grace Rainey Rogers auditorium at the Metropolitan Museum of Art, October 16, 1972. Photograph by Bill Cunningham.

"Mr. Norell was my idol. I was working alongside the master himself. I was twenty-five years old. He was seventy-two. Once, when we were lifting double-breasted wool jersey suits, sequined mermaid dresses, and organdy ball gowns out of tissue-lined boxes, I remember what he said as if it were yesterday. In the last box was a midnight blue tulle gown, sequined with twinkling silver stars. As he picked up the dazzling gown, he turned to me and with that deep raspy voice said, 'You know, Mike, designing has been good to me. It never made me rich, but it's all I ever wanted to do.'"

— Michael Vollbracht

A signature Norell siren: slim, sequined, and soigné, 1971. Drawing by Michael Vollbracht.

HONORS: ACKNOWLEDGING A LEADER

T he first Coty American Fashion Critic Award was won by Norman Norell in 1943. It was the Oscar of the fashion business. The ceremony was staged in the main hall of the Metropolitan Museum of Art and Mayor Fiorello La Guardia was there to do homage to Norell and a growing fashion industry. Paris had always been the mover and shaker of the fashion world, but with the Second World War going on, there was no room for creativity. American designers picked up the slack and began to realize that they could create their own re-envisioned industry.

Norell was lauded for the trends he started during wartime: his sequined cocktail dresses (sequins were not made of metal and therefore not affected by rationing restrictions); his cloth coats that were lined with fur; and his beloved chemise dresses, which used only half the fabric a normal Norell cocktail dress would have used.

Norell was to earn two more Coty Awards in the coming years: a return award in 1951 and, in 1956, a Coty Hall of Fame Award, its highest order.

Subsequently, Norell was covered with laurels: an honorary Doctor of Fine Arts degree from Pratt Institute in 1962, and in 1963 the International Fashion Award from the *Sunday Times* of London. The Council of Fashion Designers of America, of which Norell was president, organized a party in his honor at the Metropolitan Club in 1967. And a supper dance was given at Bonwit Teller just before his Norell perfume was launched. The first successful perfume launched in America under a designer's name cost fifty dollars per ounce and it sold one million dollars worth in its first year. Norell described it perfectly: a "new floral with green overtones—not the heavy, vampy, femme-fatale-y kind of thing. It's pleasant and has a kick to it."

Norell's Coty Award emblazoned at the base with his name and the years of his three wins: 1943, the award's inaugural year; 1951, a Return Award for the designer; and 1956, a Hall of Fame Award.

THE MASTER CLASS

Norell was a born mentor, and one of his favorite roles was taking part in the Critic's Design Program at Parsons School of Design. Only the most prestigious designers in the country were chosen to advise seniors on their all-important projects. The program was three-pronged: first, the critic would meet with his student and together they would select the best sketch from a pre-edited group of sketches to work from; the second session consisted of looking closely at the muslin version of the design and suggesting fabric and trim. And the third and final session was for studying the basted garment in the selected fabric and making any final adjustments to the fit.

Norell was also a multitalented teacher, enormously generous with his students in terms of his knowledge, his time, and his money. The kids would find some beautiful silks or wools that they desperately wanted to use and, of course, the cost was usually something well beyond their means. So Norell would anonymously purchase the fabric and have it delivered to the students without letting them know how it got there. Or sometimes he would give them some of his fine French or Italian fabrics, straight from his own workrooms. Every aspect of his students' progress was of interest, right down to the last button: occasionally, an unsuspecting student would receive a telephone call from Norell, with his slightly raspy voice, saying, "You know, Jeff, I really like what you are doing with that jacket, but I wonder if you might have thought about making it double-breasted?" Norell was vitally interested in his students' work and, in turn, his students were totally inspired and motivated by him.

For the twenty consecutive years that Norell participated in the Critic's Program, he missed only one in-person session and that was because he had cancer of the throat and was in the hospital recovering from a serious laryngectomy. He had his nurse call Parsons to ask that all the student's sketches be delivered to him at the

Student Deanna Cohen Littell (right) adds last-minute touches to the dress she designed that earned her the Norman Norell Golden Thimble Award at Parsons School of Design in 1960. Norell, left, was her proud mentor.

hospital and when he received them, he resolutely critiqued every single one, scribbling all his comments on the sketches. He couldn't speak a word at the time, but he was determined to share his advice.

Deanna Littell, class of 1960, was thrilled to learn that Norell would be working with her on her critic's project. She remembers:

> It was a totally wonderful experience, working with Mr. Norell. I chose to design an elegant trench coat over a slinky, bias-cut, white satin dress whose top wrapped around the neck like an ascot, leaving a bare back. It was an ambitious project and far more complicated than I had imagined.
>
> Mr. Norell asked me what kind of fabric I wanted to use and I told him that I was thinking of organdy, khaki organdy. Not exactly a household item! I searched for it in Norell's workroom to no avail, and finally, he sent me to Max Bernegger, a Swiss textile man. Mr. Norell called Max and said, "Give her anything she wants!" He was unbelievably generous in every way.
>
> When I thought my work was nearly done, Mr. Norell asked, "What are the details? What kind of belt and buckle?" I had thought the belt should be similar to the belt on a real raincoat, but my critic shook his head and said, "No, it needs to be something chic and elegant." Mr. Norell suggested we get buttons from Paris and insisted that we use hand-sewn buttons.
>
> I had never created real button holes before, but Mr. Norell had insisted that I make them by hand with circle stitches that go around. It wasn't easy. In our final session, I had to baste the hem and finalize the fittings on our model. Mr. Norell arrived, bearing my beautiful buttons with him and wearing a big smile.

Above: Norell, seated at left, reviewing Michael Vollbracht's bridal model in a critique at Parsons School of Design. Vollbracht is standing at right. Opposite: The organdy bridal dress that won Vollbracht the Norman Norell Golden Thimble Award in 1968. Drawing by Michael Vollbracht. Overleaf: Norell surrounded by looks he selected for his 1972 retrospective show, some of which date back to the 1930s.

TRAILBLAZER IN THE HISTORY OF AMERICAN FASHION

Born in the first year of the twentieth century, Norell was a trailblazer in the nascent American fashion industry. He pioneered many firsts: the first American designer to have his own name on a dress label; the first American designer to have his name emblazoned on a fabulously successful fragrance; and the first American designer to make clothes whose quality was truly on a par with the legendary Paris couturiers.

Norell brought his own pursuit of perfection to America, not only in the design of his clothing but also in the unstintingly high standards by which they were made. The American "rag trade," long the stepchild of the fashion world, was forever changed by Norell's efforts, not just his attitude toward clothing but also his leadership roles as the first president of the Council of Fashion Designers of America (CFDA) and the first Coty Award winner. Norell single-handedly boosted America's fashion image, with his excellence in design and his activism as a strong leader.

Stan Herman—past president of the CFDA who views Norell as his "father figure in fashion"—notes, "In the '50s, there were few American designers who were aspirational. All the talent seemed to come from Europe.… And then there was Norell—a mythical figure who started building the blocks that began to secure our country as a fashion destination. With no wasted strokes, he dressed his customer with elegance and confidence. It was all in the proportions and the restraint. The glamour is not a veneer—its layers run deep. His legacy is assured."

Think of it: fifty years, day in and day out, the designer worked at his craft, creating spectacular and flattering clothes that made all of his ladies look and feel beautiful. Norell's long legacy will always be one of simplicity and finesse, showcasing beautifully made American clothes that could rival any of those made in Europe. And the women who wore, indeed cherished, his clothes for decades can attest to that. The classic nature of their designs still commands very high prices on the vintage market, if and when they ever come up. Norman Norell made America a world-class player, and that status has remained constant to this very day.

AFTERWORD

COLLECTING NORELL

BY KENNETH POOL

Norell—the name alone says it all: glamour, simplicity, and class. I had always admired the refined and beautiful clothes that Norman Norell designed over his long career, but this was my first time bidding at an auction, and I was a little nervous. The small gallery that housed the auction had quite a large number of pieces and I had set my heart on a gorgeous pink faille cape with a large ruffle at the hem that was very dramatic, but there was no guarantee that I would get it. There were a few other interested bidders but I managed to outbid them, and in that one moment, I began a love affair with collecting Norells. I had not been a collector until the moment I raised my paddle, but in the twenty-five years since then, I have amassed a private collection of almost one hundred samples that range from perfectly cut coats and suits to the most glamorous dresses and gowns.

Norell was often referred to as America's twentieth-century Balenciaga. His tailoring was perfection, the quality of his fabric was unsurpassed, and the message that he sent out was that Seventh Avenue could be just as elegant as Paris. Starting in the 1920s, Norell designed for several companies, but I chose to draw my collection strictly from the period spanning 1960 to 1972, the years that Norell operated on his own. Not only did he design every garment, he handled the production of every piece. Norell had such a great understanding of the inner construction of a garment and a sense of proportion and color that his clothing seems to have life even on a hanger. In fact, what appealed to me most was the fact that his coats and dresses and gowns are *so* timeless, they seem to have an *infinite* life. Consider this: in 2010, Michelle Obama, wife of President Barack Obama, chose to wear a 1950s Norell black lace overlay, full-skirted dress to the "Christmas in Washington" concert. Timeless is the word, indeed!

Pale pink silk faille ruffled cape, early 1960s. The cape was Kenneth Pool's first vintage Norell purchase as a collector.

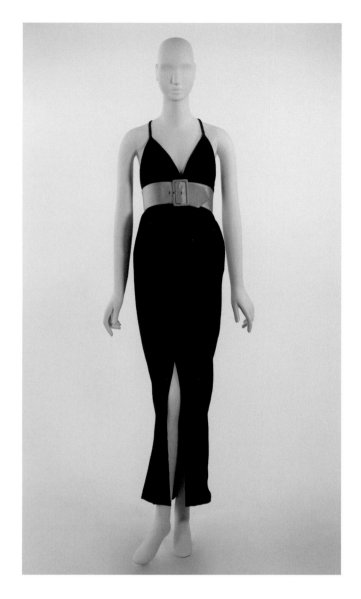

One of the most exciting aspects for me of being a collector is the "hunt." There are all manner of shops and vintage clothing stores throughout the country. I have acquired some pieces from Europe, and of course I love the thrill of finding a treasure on the Internet. Once I find something I really want, I check to see if it is documented by researching vintage magazines and store advertisements, and the many extraordinary editorial pages that were graced by Norell's designs in *Vogue* and *Harper's Bazaar*, and photographed by Richard Avedon, Bert Stern, and Irving Penn, three of the most highly regarded photographers in the world.

As a designer myself, who has been in this business for over twenty-five years, I know that Norell's influence can still be seen in today's styles, especially in coats and simple dress designs. I am always thrilled to rescue the pieces that I purchase and I take great joy in being able to show them to friends and educate them about this man and his extraordinary talents.

The strict vision and dedication to his craft made Norell a highly respected designer, not only in America but also in Europe. His designs, even if elaborate, are based on a calm and well-proportioned silhouette. It is an enormous pleasure for me to collect and share his beautiful and everlasting designs.

Above: Black wool jersey gown inspired by John Singer Sargent's *Madame X*, with crisscrossed back and ice-blue satin belt, Spring 1967. Opposite: Prussian-blue Pilgrim-collar wool coat with black buttons, Fall 1968.

"For half a century, women have treasured their Norells as if they were emeralds or Renoirs. They wear them lovingly for years, content that they're dressed in the best that money can buy, then pack them away respectfully because they can't bear to part with them. A Norell dress never seems to wear out."

—Bernadine Morris, *The New York Times*, October 15, 1972

Norell, the master, adds his final flourishes to the model in her slinky black-sequin cocktail dress, glammed up with silky coq feathers at neck and hem and topped off with a jazzy little coq-feathered cloche. On with the show! 1965. Photograph by Jacques Ducrot.

ACKNOWLEDGMENTS

This book might never have happened had we not been introduced to Lawrence Abrams, something of a self-taught Norell scholar, almost from the time he could speak. Fashion was in his genes: his mother, Miriam, was involved with the design industry for many years and was both a friend and an associate of Norell. When Lawrence was young and school was over for the day, his mother brought him to work, exposing him to the world of fashion. No one could have absorbed more than he did. His knowledge of Norell's *modus operandi* is keen, and his impressive understanding of the technical side of the master's mind is impressive. Lawrence grew up poring over *Women's Wear Daily*, and we are certain he has never forgotten anything he read in it. He is a virtual encyclopedia of Norelliana and has been very generous in sharing his expertise and stories for which we are enormously grateful.

There is no one working in American fashion today who understands the artistry of dressmaking more than Ralph Rucci. The authors are so thankful that he was able to write such an insightful and poetic foreword to our book.

Marc Fowler's beautiful and illuminating original photography is a very special grace note in this book, as are the skillful and magician-like restorations he undertook for long-damaged images.

Kenneth Pool's graciousness in allowing us to photograph his Norell collection and his thoughtful perceptions into Norell's clothing were, and are, invaluable.

Max Bernegger — whose business acumen helped shape Norell's company and whose cheerful encouragement, gift of sharing Norell stories, and extraordinary historical recall during our myriad long telephone chats — contributed greatly to this work.

Michael Vollbracht's brilliant illustrations and keen memory of Norell served as a shining beacon for us from day one.

We thank the Taunton Press for its permission to reprint excerpts from an article about Norman Norell, "Class All the Way," by Mary C. Elliott, which was published in its *Threads* magazine in September 1989. Mrs. Elliott was an instructor and the curator of historical textiles at Mount Mary College in Milwaukee, Wisconsin.

Thanks to Philip Reeser, our steadfast editor, who championed this book from the very first pitch and steered it to its beautiful conclusion; Phil Kovacevich, who stylishly and gracefully designed this book with a deft hand and a great sense of humor; and Charles Miers, our publisher, who, once convinced of our passion for the subject matter, continually pushed us all to new heights.

And to the many people who have helped bring this book to life, the authors also wish to thank the following: Betty Halbreich, Ellin Saltzman, Steven Kolb, Eric Rachlis, Patricia Mears, Denise Linden, Phyllis Magidsen, Robert Riggs, Adrien Arpel, John Calcagno, Philippe de La Chapelle, Michael Ward, Paul Alexander, Johnny Walker, Donald Loftus, Pat Werblin, Emma Gardner, Vals Osborne, Fred Dennis, Elizabeth Way, Jeff Roth, Vanessa Friedman, Phyllis Collazo, Lori Reese, Megan Conway, Anne M. Young, Joshua Greene, Shawn Penrod, Michael Avedon, James Martin, Erin Harris, Valerie Steele, Abel Rapp, Tom Fallon, Carla LaMonte, Sassa Osborne, Jano Herbosch, Stan Herman, Deanna Littell, Jeannene Booher, Vicky Tiel, Sue Davidson Lowe, Karin Jacobs, Pat Peterson, Jean Rosenberg, Bob Steele, Marcia Schaeffer, Mary Fisher, Fred Dennis, Karen Trivette, Dr. Kevin Cahill, Sondra Zaharias, and Allison Ingram.

Every effort has been made to locate copyright holders of photographs and other imagery included in this book. Credit, if and as available, is provided below. Errors or omissions in credit citations, or failure to obtain permission if required by copyright law, have been either unavoidable or unintentional. The authors, editor, and publisher welcome any information that would allow them to correct future reprints.

Kees van Dongen, *Marchesa Casati* © 2017 Artists Rights Society (ARS), New York / ADAGP, Paris: 4, 163, 170–71

Photograph by Milton H. Greene © 2017 Joshua Greene: 2–3, 4, 60–61, 71, 170–71, 197 (upper left)

Drawing by Kenneth Paul Block. From the Collection of Max Bernegger: 6, 46, 70, 166

Horst P. Horst / *Vogue*, March 15, 1961 © Condé Nast: 8

The New School Archives and Special Collections, The New School, New York, NY: 11, 15 (left and right), 66, 90–91, 183

New York Post Archives / *The New York Post* / Getty Images: 12

Bert Stern / Condé Nast Collection / Getty Images: 14, 164–65

Bert Stern / *Vogue*, March 1, 1963 © Condé Nast: 16–17

Bill Aller / *The New York Times* / Redux: 18

Harper's Bazaar cover, March 1, 1950 / Photograph by Louise Dahl-Wolfe. Collection Center for Creative Photography © 1989 Center for Creative Photography, Arizona Board of Regents: 21

Gjon Mili / The LIFE Picture Collection / Getty Images: 22, 23

Photographs of Kenneth Pool Collection © Marc Fowler: 26, 29, 30, 31, 34, 35, 37, 39, 41, 51, 55, 75, 76, 78, 79 (left and right), 80 (left and right), 81, 82, 83, 87, 144, 157, 158, 167, 168–69, 216, 218 (left and right), 219

© Michael Vollbracht / Courtesy of The New School Archives and Special Collections, The New School, New York, NY: 28, 62, 72, 194, 206, 213

Horst P. Horst / *Vogue*, October 1, 1952 © Condé Nast: 32–33

From the collection of Max Bernegger: 38, 99, 117, 141, 160, 196

Horst P. Horst / Condé Nast Collection / Getty Images: 42–43, 45, 56–57, 148–49, 178–79

John Rawlings / Condé Nast Collection / Getty Images: 47, 111, 134

Irving Penn / *Vogue*, September 15, 1952 © Condé Nast: 48–49

Irving Penn / *Vogue*, April 1, 1968 © Condé Nast: 52–53

Courtesy of Photofest: 59

Bettmann / Getty Images: 63, 138, 161, 163, 182, 186 (left), 197 (upper right)

Tony Palmieri / Penske Media / REX / Shutterstock: 64, 181

John Rawlings / *Vogue*, March 1, 1946 © Condé Nast: 67

Irving Penn / *Vogue*, April 1, 1972 © Condé Nast: 68

John Rawlings / *Vogue*, September 1, 1943 © Condé Nast: 69

Gianni Penati / *Vogue*, September 15, 1971 © Condé Nast: 73

Norman Norell. The New School Archives and Special Collections, The New School, New York, NY: 74, 84, 86, 89

© Leo Friedman: 92–93

Courtesy of the *New York Times*: 96, 197 (bottom)

Indianapolis Museum of Art, Gift of John Moore, 1985.547 © Norman Norell: 100 (left)

Indianapolis Museum of Art, Gift of John Moore, 1985.544 © Norman Norell: 100 (right)

Indianapolis Museum of Art, Gift of John Moore, 1985.539 © Norman Norell: 101

Pictorial Press Ltd / Alamy Stock Photo: 102

Sunset Boulevard / Corbis Historical / Getty Images: 103, 187 (upper left)

William Eckenberg / *The New York Times* / Redux: 104

© Michael Vollbracht: 105

Sketch by Hattie Carnegie / From the Collections of the Museum of the City of New York: 106

John Springer Collection / Corbis Historical / Getty Images: 107

New York Daily News Archive / *New York Daily News* / Getty Images: 110

John Rawlings / *Vogue*, February 1, 1945 © Condé Nast: 112–13

Photograph by William Helburn: 114

John Rawlings / *Vogue*, February 1, 1944 © Condé Nast: 115

John Rawlings / *Vogue*, May 15, 1942 © Condé Nast: 119

Genevieve Naylor / Corbis Historical / Getty Images: 120–21

© The Cecil Beaton Studio Archive at Sotheby's: 123

Erwin Blumenfeld / *Vogue*, March 15, 1950 © Condé Nast: 125

John Rawlings / *Vogue*, October 15, 1957 © Condé Nast: 126

Irving Penn / *Vogue*, March 1, 1958 © Condé Nast: 127

John Rawlings / *Vogue*, March 1, 1944 © Condé Nast: 129

Carl Oscar August Erickson / *Vogue*, May 15, 1954 © Condé Nast: 130

© The Estate of Erwin Blumenfeld: 131

Erwin Blumenfeld / *Vogue*, September 1, 1954 © Condé Nast: 133

Karen Radkai / *Vogue*, October 15, 1955 / © Condé Nast: 135

Betty Threat, Wildenstein Galleries, New York, NY, 1943 / Photograph by Louise Dahl-Wolfe. Collection Center for Creative Photography © 1989 Center for Creative Photography, Arizona Board of Regents: 136

Serge Balkin / Condé Nast Collection / Getty Images: 137

© Mark Shaw / mptvimages.com: 143

© Marc Fowler: 150, 208

Courtesy of Jeffrey Banks: 152

Photograph by James Moore for *Harper's Bazaar*: 153

Irving Penn / *Vogue*, February 1, 1967 © Condé Nast: 154, 155

Bob Stone / *Vogue*, October 15, 1972 © Condé Nast: 159

The Francesco Scavullo Foundation. The Francesco Scavullo Trust: 172.

Jack Mitchell / Corbis Premium Historical / Getty Images: 176

Michael Ochs Archive / Getty Images: 180

Klute (1971) © Warner Bros. / Courtesy of Photofest / page 184

Silver Screen Collection / Moviepix / Getty Images: 185 (left)

The Wheeler Dealers (1963) © MGM / Courtesy of Photofest: 185 (right)

Courtesy of Phyllis McGuire: 186 (right)

Ron Galella / Ron Galella Collection / Getty Images: 187 (lower left)

AP Images / Manuel Balce Ceneta: page 187 (right)

Cher, Los Angeles, January 23, 1972 / Photograph by Richard Avedon © The Richard Avedon Foundation: 189

Sal Traina / Penske Media / REX / Shutterstock: 190

CBS Photo Archive / Getty Images: 191

Judy Garland, New York, January 7, 1963 / Photograph by Richard Avedon © The Richard Avedon Foundation: 193

Photograph by Bill Cunningham. Courtesy of the William Clegg Agency: 200, 204–05

Joseph Scherschel / The LIFE Picture Collection / Getty Images: 210

Courtesy of Michael Vollbracht: 212

Wilbur Pippin / *Vogue*, October 15, 1972 © Condé Nast: 214–15

Photograph by Jerome Ducrot. Courtesy of the *New York Times*: 221

This book is dedicated to Frank Rizzo, former dean of fashion at Parsons School of Design, who not only fostered my passion for Norell and his clothing but also wholeheartedly encouraged me before his untimely death to write this book. I am eternally grateful to him.

—Jeffrey Banks

First published in the United States of America in 2018 by

Rizzoli Electa

A division of Rizzoli International Publications, Inc.

300 Park Avenue South

New York, New York 10010

www.rizzoliusa.com

ISBN: 978-0-8478-6124-8

Library of Congress Control Number: 2017951865

Philip Reeser, Editor

Barbara Sadick, Production Manager

Megan Conway, Copy Editor

Design by Phil Kovacevich

Printed and bound in China

2018 2019 2020 2021 / 10 9 8 7 6 5 4 3 2 1

Pages 2–3: Elegant and sportive daytime outfits in brilliant fall colors against the backdrop of Belmont Race Track, 1960. Photograph by Milton H. Greene.

Page 4: Norman Norell with some of his favored models in variations of the designer's mermaid dress — one of his classic hallmarks — in front of Norell's Kees van Dongen painting that inspired their 1920s look. Gorgeous jewel-colored paillettes, from left, skinny-strapped red gown, long-sleeved silver gown, color-blocked gold and silver gown, and beaded multicolored paisley gown, 1960. Photograph by Milton H. Greene.

Page 6: Two views of Norell's tangerine wool double-breasted theater suit, with black wool jersey halter-top dress, satin bow at the waist, early 1960s. Drawing by Kenneth Paul Block.